T0336821

Systems Architecture Modeling with the Arcadia Method

Implementation of Model Based System Engineering Set

coordinated by
Pascal Roques

Systems Architecture Modeling with the Arcadia Method

A Practical Guide to Capella

Pascal Roques

First published 2018 in Great Britain and the United States by ISTE Press Ltd and Elsevier Ltd

Apart from any fair dealing for the purposes of research or private study, or criticism or review, as permitted under the Copyright, Designs and Patents Act 1988, this publication may only be reproduced, stored or transmitted, in any form or by any means, with the prior permission in writing of the publishers, or in the case of reprographic reproduction in accordance with the terms and licenses issued by the CLA. Enquiries concerning reproduction outside these terms should be sent to the publishers at the undermentioned address:

ISTE Press Ltd
27-37 St George's Road
London SW19 4EU
UK

www.iste.co.uk

Elsevier Ltd
The Boulevard, Langford Lane
Kidlington, Oxford, OX5 1GB
UK

www.elsevier.com

Notices
Knowledge and best practice in this field are constantly changing. As new research and experience broaden our understanding, changes in research methods, professional practices, or medical treatment may become necessary.

Practitioners and researchers must always rely on their own experience and knowledge in evaluating and using any information, methods, compounds, or experiments described herein. In using such information or methods they should be mindful of their own safety and the safety of others, including parties for whom they have a professional responsibility.

To the fullest extent of the law, neither the Publisher nor the authors, contributors, or editors, assume any liability for any injury and/or damage to persons or property as a matter of products liability, negligence or otherwise, or from any use or operation of any methods, products, instructions, or ideas contained in the material herein.

For information on all our publications visit our website at http://store.elsevier.com/

© ISTE Press Ltd 2018
The rights of Pascal Roques to be identified as the author of this work have been asserted by him in accordance with the Copyright, Designs and Patents Act 1988.

British Library Cataloguing-in-Publication Data
A CIP record for this book is available from the British Library
Library of Congress Cataloging in Publication Data
A catalog record for this book is available from the Library of Congress
ISBN 978-1-78548-168-0

Printed and bound in the UK and US

Contents

Foreword

The Arcadia method appeared during the year 2007 as part of the Thales Airborne Systems: this structured engineering method, which aimed to define and validate the architectural design of complex systems, was immediately followed by the Melody Advance tool, which aided its implementation.

The method has since demonstrated its benefits in all of Thales' areas of excellence (Defense, Space, Aeronautics, Land transport, Security, etc.) providing structure to the collaborative work of those involved, who are often numerous during the definition phase of the system. The Arcadia method and the Melody Advance tool have progressively been deployed within the Group, and later externally. After going public, Melody Advance entered the world of Open Source software, under the name Capella.

Pascal has followed this deployment since the early stages of the project, and his collaboration with Thales University, which started 10 years ago, continues to this day, namely in the form of training that he provides on the Arcadia method and the Melody Advance/Capella tool.

Capella provides specific solutions to the problems of System Engineers and System Architects. It allows for the construction and maintenance of global and coherent systemic visions that integrate operational, system, logical and physical views, as well as the associated viewpoints of all stakeholders.

This book will allow you to experience Capella, and there is nothing better for this than a practical case... As Albert Einstein said:

"Knowledge is experience, everything else is just information".

The example that illustrates all of the aspects involved in the implementation of Capella is EOLE, a balloon probe system whose main goal is to provide meteorological data to different types of users. It is representative through:

– its multiple stakeholders and user types;

– its various types of component (hardware, software, etc.);

– its types of functional and non-functional requirements.

It is this same case study that highlights the training provided by Thales University, which puts trainees very quickly into concrete situations.

Since 2008, Pascal has trained more than 1,200 Thales employees in the different sites in France and Europe (more than 100 sessions). It is this passion and his qualities as a teacher that will guide you throughout this logical and structured application of Capella.

So jump right in and follow Pascal in the fascinating experience of modeling.

Odile MORNAS
Thales Global Services
INCOSE ESEP Certified

Preface

Aims of this book

The Arcadia modeling method was designed by Thales for its own needs. Since 2011 it has been applied to a growing number of projects over a variety of domains (avionic, rail systems, defense systems in all environments, satellite systems and ground stations, communication systems, etc.) and in many different countries.

This method is supported in its modeling aspect by a dedicated tool that responds to the constraints present during full-scale deployment in an operating context. This tool, called Capella (Melody Advance internally in Thales), is currently available free of charge for the system engineering community as an Open Source solution (www.polarsys.org/capella/).

My goal in this work is the introduction of this new environment for modeling in system engineering. Based on my experience as a modeling consultant in a number of domains, my pedagogical experience as an UML and SysML trainer for over 15 years, and as a provider of training with Melody Advance within the Thales group (more than 120 training sessions in France and in Europe, more than 1,500 trainees), I hope to show the advantages and assets of the Capella tool based on the Arcadia method.

This book is first of all aimed at system engineering professionals, those who are in charge of complex systems, both material and software, whether in the domains of aeronautics, space, energy, transport, defense, automotive, etc.

Structure of the book

Chapter 1 constitutes a reminder of the Arcadia method, described in detail in another book from the same series: "Model-based System and Architecture Engineering with the Arcadia Method" [VOI 18].

Chapter 2 presents the stakes and principles involved with the Capella tool, which implements the Arcadia method. First, we shall establish the perimeter that is targeted by the tool, as well as its origin. Next we shall describe the principles behind the human–machine interface, as well as the varying nature of the diagrams involved.

Chapters 3–7 demonstrate concrete use of the Capella tool (and therefore also the Arcadia method) in a realistic case study from Operational Analysis to EPBS. The difficulty in system engineering is often finding a case study that is representative enough, but not too complex or too specific to a single technical domain. In the context of this book, we have reused and adapted an example that we used over a hundred times during Capella training sessions carried out first at Thales, and later outside of Thales.

The conclusion provides a summary of the important points regarding the Capella tool and presents its "under construction" ecosystem mainly based on the collaborative project Clarity (www.clarity-se.org/) and the future Capella IC (*Industry Consortium*).

Acknowledgments

This work would doubtless not have seen the light of day without the support of the Clarity project, as part of which I was asked to write a book on the Capella tool, with the objective of spreading awareness about it. A big thanks first of all to Daniel Exertier (Thales Corporate) for involving me in this adventure, and to all the others from Thales with whom I have worked over the course of these many years as a trainer with the internal tool Melody Advance. While there are too many to name all of them here, I would like to thank in particular Jean-Luc Voirin (Thales Airborne Systems) and Stéphane Bonnet (Thales Corporate); Philippe Lugagne, Stéphanie Cheutin and Laetitia Saoud (Thales Alenia Space in Toulouse); as well as Patricia Pancher and Odile Mornas (Thales University).

Thank you to my technical proofreaders for their astute comments:

– *Olivier Casse (expert in embedded system modeling languages and tools, veteran of I-Logix/Telelogic and Atego/Artisan);*

– *Jérôme Montigny (Capella evangelist with Continental Automotive in Toulouse);*

– *Benoit Viaud (Clarity project member with Artal in Toulouse).*

Pascal ROQUES
October 2017

Reminders for the Arcadia Method

1.1. Novelties, strengths and principles

1.1.1. *History*

System engineers have been making use of modeling techniques for a long time. Structured analysis and design technique (SADT) and structured analysis for real time (SA/RT) are some of the best known of these, and date back to the 1980s. There are many other approaches based on Petri nets or finite state machines. However, these techniques are also limited by their range and expressivity, as well as by the difficulty in integrating them with other formalisms and with requirements.

The rise of UML [ROQ 04] in the world of software and the industrial effort toward developing the tools that accompany it have naturally led to its use being considered in system engineering. However, due to a design process that was strongly influenced by its intended use in object programming, the language was, at least in the early versions, not particularly adapted to modeling complex systems, and was therefore not well suited to system engineering.

An interesting attempt was the publication of a UML variant for system engineering in 2006–2007. This new language, called SysML [CAS 18], was strongly inspired by version 2 of UML, but added the possibility of representing system requirements, non-software elements (mechanical, hydraulic, sensors, etc.), physical equations, continuous flows (matter, energy, etc.) and allocations. Unfortunately, in practice it has been shown that the filiation of the SysML language to UML often leads to difficulty in terms of comprehension and use for system engineers who are not also computer scientists.

This is the reason that led Thales to define the Arcadia method [VOI 16, VOI 17], along with its underlying formalism, for its own needs. It has been applied since 2011 in a growing number of projects across a great variety of domains (avionics, railway systems, defense systems in all fields, air traffic control, command control, area surveillance, complex sensor systems, satellite systems and ground stations, communications systems, etc.), and in many countries (France, Germany, United Kingdom, Italy, Australia, Canada, etc.).

The modeling aspect of the method is supported by a dedicated tool that responds to the constraints involved with full-scale application in an operational context. This tool, called Capella (Melody Advance internally at Thales), is currently freely available for the engineering community as an Open Source application.

1.1.2. *Founding principles*

Today's complex systems are limited by a number of requirements or constraints, often concurrently, and sometimes contradictorily: functional requirements (services expected by the users), and non-functional requirements (security, operating safety, mass, scalability, cost, etc.). The initial engineering phases of such systems are critical as they condition the aptitude of the architecture used to answer the needs of the clients, as well as the proper distribution of the requirements toward the components, arising from the architecture used. In order to properly handle delays and costs, it is vital to be able to verify the adequacy of the solution with regard to needs from the system design phase, and to minimize the risk of coming across limitations of the solution – thus jeopardizing the architecture – at a more or less advanced stage of development, or even during integration or qualification of the system.

Current practice in systems engineering in the last few years has made use (and rightly so) of a formalization of needs and expectations expressed by the client, in the form of textual requirements, which are then traced (manually) during realization to justify them in relation to the client needs. The limitations of this approach arise mainly from the fact that non-formalized, textual requirements make it harder to verify their coherence and their completeness. Moreover, they are confined to the expression of need and are therefore poorly adapted to describing the solution and to mastering its complexity, or to structuring the engineering. This is one of the reasons that led Thales to the development and deployment of an innovative approach called Arcadia.

Arcadia is a structured engineering method aimed at defining and validating the architecture of complex systems. It favors collaborative work between all stakeholders – of which there are often many – involved in the engineering (or definition) phase of the system. It allows for iterations to be carried out from the definition phase that will help converge the architecture toward congruence with all of the needs identified.

Textual requirements are still present and used as a main contribution toward expressing need at the start of the engineering process. As such, Arcadia takes its place as a major support for engineering and its control, relying on a formalization of the analysis of need, whether operational, functional, or non-functional (functions expected of the system, functional chains, etc.), and on the definition/justification of the architecture based on this functional analysis.

The general principles of Arcadia are the following:

– all of the engineering stakeholders share the same methodology, the same information, the same description of the need and the product in the form of a shared model;

– each specialized type of engineering (for example security, performance, cost and mass) is formalized as a "viewpoint" in relation to the requirements from which the proposed architecture is then verified;

– the rules for the anticipated verification of the architecture are established in order to verify the architecture as soon as possible;

– co-engineering between the different levels of engineering is supported by the joint elaboration of models, and the models of the different levels and specialties are deducted/validated/linked one to the other.

To summarize, Arcadia possesses innovative characteristics that are yet to be properly demonstrated in its domain:

– it covers all of the structuring activities of engineering, from capturing the operational needs of the client to integration/verification/validation (IVV);

– it takes into account the multiple levels of engineering, as well as the efficient collaboration between them (system, subsystem, software, hardware, etc.);

– it integrates coengineering with specialty engineering types (security, safety, performance, interfaces, logistics, etc.) and of IVV;

– it is based on the use of models that are not only descriptive, but also able to validate the definition and the properties of the architecture, and that constitute the main support for coengineering between the teams involved;

– it has successfully passed the test of applicability in real-size projects and in constrained operational situations, as it is currently being used in several dozen large projects in various divisions (and countries) of Thales.

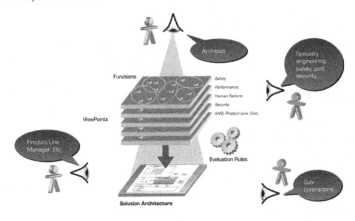

Figure 1.1. *Coengineering with Arcadia*

1.2. Architecture levels and associated concepts

1.2.1. *Overview*

NOTE.– The vocabulary that we shall explain in the following sections is the one used in version 1.1 of the Capella tool.

The different working levels of Arcadia are the following:

– OPERATIONAL ANALYSIS: "What the users of the system need to accomplish":

- analysis of the issues of operational users by identifying the actors that must interact with the system, their activities and their interactions with each other.

– ANALYSIS OF THE SYSTEM NEEDS: "What the system has to accomplish for the users":

- external functional analysis as a response to identify the system functions needed by its users (e.g. "calculate the optimal path" and "detect a threat"), limited by the non-functional properties asked for.

– LOGICAL ARCHITECTURE: "How the system will work to fulfill expectations":

- internal functional system analysis: which are the subfunctions that must be carried out and put together to establish the "user" functions identified during the previous stage;

- identification of the logical components that carry out these internal subfunctions, by integrating the non-functional constraints that we choose to deal with at this level.

– PHYSICAL ARCHITECTURE: "How the system will be developed and built":

- the goal of this level is the same as that of the logical architecture, except that it defines the final architecture of the system as it must be created;

- it adds the functions required by the implementation and by the technical choices, and highlights behavioral components (e.g. software components) that carry out these functions. These behavioral components are then implemented using implementation components (e.g. processor board), which provide the necessary material resources.

– EPBS   (End   Product   Breakdown   Structure)   AND INTEGRATION CONTRACTS: "What is expected from the provider of each component":

- this step deduces from the physical architecture the conditions that each component must fulfill to satisfy the architecture design constraints and limitations, established in the previous phases.

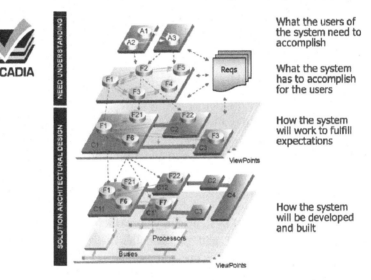

Figure 1.2. *The main engineering levels of Arcadia*

It must be noted that the method does not always have to be top-down in nature, but can also perfectly be bottom-up, for example if we start with an existing system that is to be worked on. The question relates more to architectural levels than to phases or steps.

Moreover, not all architectural levels are mandatory for all projects. Operational Analysis, Logical Architecture and EPBS are considered to be optional, depending on the complexity of the system under study and the goals of the model.

1.2.2. *Operational Analysis*

The highest level of the Arcadia method is Operational Analysis ("what the users of the future system need to accomplish"). The goal here is to focus on the identification of the needs and objectives of future users of the system in order to guarantee the adequacy of the system faced with these operational needs.

NOTE.– At this level, the system is not (yet) recognized as a modeling element. It will only be recognized as such from the System Analysis level onward.

This level can be treated as a model of the jobs of future users: what are their activities, what roles must they fulfill and under which operational scenarios?

The main concepts proposed by Arcadia at this level are as follows:

– Operational Capability: capability of an organization to provide a high level service leading to an operational objective being reached (for example Provide weather forecasts, etc.);

– Operational Entity: entity belonging to the real world (organization, existing system, etc.) whose role is to interact with the system being studied or with its users (for example Crew, Ship, etc.);

– Operational Actor: particular case of a (human) non-decomposable operational entity (for example Pilot, etc.);

– Operational Activity: process step carried out in order to reach a precise objective by an operational entity, which might need to use the future system in order to do so (for example Detect a threat, Collect meteorological data, etc.);

– Operational Interaction: exchange of information or of unidirectional matter between operational activities (for example meteorological data, etc.);

– Operational Process: series of activities and of interactions that contribute toward an operational capability.

– Operational Scenario: scenario that describes the behavior of entities and and/or operational activities in the context of an operational capability. It is commonly represented as a sequence diagram, with the vertical axis representing time.

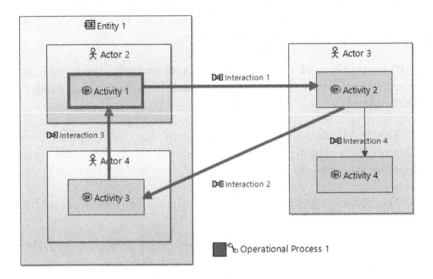

Figure 1.3. *Diagram showing the main concepts behind Operational Analysis. For a color version of the figure, see www.iste.co.uk/roques/arcadia.zip*

In Figure 1.3, first of all we can see the structural elements (gray rectangles), i.e. the Entities and the Actors. An Operational Actor is a human and non-decomposable Operational Entity. An Entity can contain other Entities or Actors, like Entity 1, which contains the Actors 2 and 4. Next, we can see the Activities (orange rectangles), within the Actors or Entities: this is the allocation relation. One or several Activities can be associated with a same Entity or Actor. This is the case with Activity 2 and Activity 4, which are associated with Actor 3. Between the Activities we can see the Interactions, or operational exchanges (orange arrows). A succession of Activities and Interactions constitutes an Operational Process. This is the case for the Operational Process 1 in the figure, which is made up of the sequences of Interactions 1–3. This Operational Process is represented both by a blue square on the diagram, and also by the bold and blue Interactions involved, as well as the source and target Activities (here the same Activity 1).

Other more advanced concepts are also available if needed: Operational Role, Communication Mean, Mode and State, Exchange Item, Class, etc. We shall discuss some of these throughout the case study presented in Chapter 3.

1.2.3. System Analysis

System Analysis involves the identification of the Capabilities and Functions of the system that will satisfy the operational needs ("what the system must accomplish for the users").

This involves carrying out an external functional analysis of the system under study in order to identify the System Functions required by the users (e.g. "calculate the optimal itinerary", "detect a threat") from the response, under the constraint of the non-functional properties ordered.

NOTE.– The System is identified as a modeling element at this level. It is a "black box" containing no other structural elements, only allocated Functions.

The main concepts proposed by Arcadia at this level are as follows:

– System: organized group of elements that function as a unit (black box) and respond to the needs of the users. The System owns Component Ports that allow it to interact with the external Actors;

– Actor: any element that is external to the System (human or non-human) that interacts with it. (for example Pilot, Test operator, etc.);

– System Capability: capability of the System to provide a high-level service allowing it to carry out an operational objective (for example provide meteorological data, etc.);

– Function: behavior or service provided by the System or by an Actor (for example detect a threat, measure altitude, etc.). A Function owns Function Ports that allow it to communicate with the other Functions. A Function can be split into subfunctions;

– Functional Exchange: unidirectional exchange of information or of matter between two Functions, linking two Function Ports;

– Component Exchange: connection between the System and one of its external Actors, allowing circulation of Functional Exchanges;

– Scenario: dynamic occurrence describing how the System and its Actors interact in the context of a System Capability. It is commonly represented in the form of a sequence diagram, with the vertical axis representing time;

– Functional Chain: element of the model that enables a specific path to be designated among all possible paths (using certain Functions and Functional Exchanges). This is particularly useful for assigning constraints (latency, criticality, etc.), as well as organizing tests.

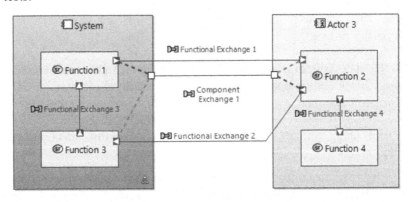

Figure 1.4. *Diagram showing the main concepts behind System Analysis. For a color version of the figure, see www.iste.co.uk/roques/arcadia.zip*

In Figure 1.4, we can first of all see the structural elements (blue rectangles), i.e. the System and the Actors. An Actor is an entity that is external to the System (human or not). Next we can see the Functions (green rectangles), which are inside the System or the Actors: this is the allocation relation. One or several Functions can be allocated to the same structural element. This is the case for Functions

2 and 4, which are allocated to Actor 3, as well as for Functions 1 and 3, which are allocated to the System. The Functional Exchanges (green arrows) are represented between the Functions, linking a Function Port of the output of a Function (green square) to a Function Port of the input of another Function (orange square). One or more Functional Exchanges can be allocated to the same Component Exchange (blue line). This is the case for Functional Exchanges 1 and 2, which are both allocated to the Component Exchange 1, as shown by the dotted line linking the Function Ports to the Component Ports. A Component Exchange has to link the System to one of its Actors, via Component Ports (white squares), which can be uni- or bidirectional. In the case of Figure 1.4, the Ports are bidirectional, since the Functional Exchanges are of opposite directions.

Other more advanced concepts are also available if needed: Mission, Mode and State, Exchange Item, Class, Interface, etc. We will discuss several of these in the context of the case study in Chapter 4.

1.2.4. *Logical Architecture*

The level of Logical Architecture aims to identify Logical Components inside the System ("how the system will work to fulfill expectations"), their relations and their content, independently of any considerations of technology or implementation.

Next an internal functional analysis of the system must be carried out: the subfunctions required to carry out the System Functions chosen during the previous phase must be identified; next, a split into Logical Components to which these internal subfunctions will be allocated must be determined, all the while integrating the non-functional constraints that have been chosen for processing at this level.

The main concepts proposed by Arcadia at this level are as follows:

– Logical Component: structural element within the System, with structural Ports to interact with the other Logical Components and the external Actors. A Logical Component can have one or more Logical Functions. It can also be subdivided into Logical subcomponents;

– Logical Actor: any element that is external to the System (human or non-human) and that interacts with it (for example Pilot, Maintenance operator, etc.).

– Logical Function: behavior or service provided by a Logical Component or by a Logical Actor. A Logical Function has Function Ports that allow it to communicate with the other Logical Functions. A Logical Function can be subdivided into Logical subfunctions;

– Functional Exchange: a unidirectional exchange of information or matter between two Logical Functions, linking two Function Ports;

– Component Exchange: connection between the Logical Components and/or the Logical Actors, allowing circulation of the Functional Exchanges;

– Logical Scenario: dynamic occurrence describing the interactions between Logical Components and Logical Actors in the context of a Capability. It is commonly represented as a sequence diagram, with the vertical axis representing the time axis;

– Functional Chain: element of the model that enables a specific path to be designated among all possible paths (using certain Functions and Functional Exchanges). This is particularly useful for assigning constraints (latency, criticality, etc.), as well as organizing tests;

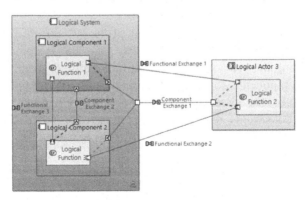

Figure 1.5. *Diagram showing the main concepts behind Logical Architecture. For a color version of the figure, see www.iste.co.uk/roques/arcadia.zip*

In Figure 1.5, we can first of all see the structural elements (blue rectangles), i.e. the Logical Components (contained in overarching box that represents the System at the Logical level) and the Actors. Next, we can see the Functions (green rectangles), within the Logical Components or the Actors: this is the allocation relation. The Functional Exchanges are represented between the Functions, always linking a Function Port from a Function output to a Function Port from the input of another Function. A Component Exchange either links the Logical System to one of its Actors, or a Logical Component directly to an external Actor, or two Logical Components via Component Ports (uni- or bidirectional). In the case of Figure 1.5, the Ports of Component Exchange 2 that link the two Logical Components inside the System are unidirectional, since only one Functional Exchange is allocated to it. On the other hand, Component Exchange 1, which still links Actor 3 to the System, is now delegated to the two Logical Components via unidirectional Component Ports, each belonging to a different Logical Component. This mechanism allows us to finely specify the responsibilities of each Logical Component by attaching it to the responsibilities of the System level.

Other more advanced concepts are also available if needed: Mission, Mode and State, Exchange Item, Class, Interface, etc. We shall discuss some of these during the case study presented in Chapter 5.

1.2.5. *Physical Architecture*

The objective of this level is the same as for Logical Architecture, except that it defines the final architecture of the system, and how it must be carried out ("how the system will be built").

It adds the Functions required for implementation, as well as the technical choices, and highlights two types of Physical Component:

– Behavior Physical Component: Physical Component tasked with Physical Functions and therefore carrying out part of the behavior of the System (for example software component, data server, etc.);

– Node (or Implementation) Physical Component: Physical Component that provides the material resources needed for one or several Behavior Components (for example processor, router, OS, etc.).

At this level, the main concepts proposed by Arcadia are similar to those of the Logical Architecture: Physical Function, Functional Exchange, Physical Component, Physical Actor, etc. However, there are some additional concepts, notably:

– Physical Port: non-oriented port that belongs to an Implementation Component (or Node). The structural port (Component Port), on the other hand, has to belong to a Behavior Component;

– Physical Link: non-oriented material connection between Implementation Components (or Nodes). The Component Exchange remains a connection between Behavior Components. A Physical Link allows one or several Component Exchanges to take place (for example Ethernet cable, USB cable, etc.);

– Physical Path: organized succession of Physical Links enabling a Component Exchange to go through several Implementation Components (or Nodes).

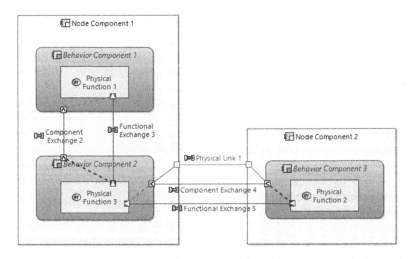

Figure 1.6. *Diagram showing the main concepts behind Physical Architecture. For a color version of the figure, see www.iste.co.uk/roques/arcadia.zip*

In Figure 1.6, we can first of all see the Node Components (yellow rectangles). Next, we can see the Behavior Components (blue rectangles) deployed over each Node. Finally, we can see the Functions (green rectangles) inside the Behavior Components: this is the allocation relation. The Functional Exchanges are represented between the Functions, always linking a Function Port from a Function output to a Function Port from the input of another Function. A Component Exchange links either a Behavior Physical Component to an external Actor, or two Behavior Physical Components, via Component Ports (uni or bidirectional). One or more Functional Exchanges can be allocated to the same Component Exchange. Next, the Component Exchanges can themselves pass through Physical Links (red lines), linking two Physical Ports (yellow squares) of Node Components. This is the case in Figure 1.6, where Functional Exchange 5 is allocated to Component Exchange 4, which passes through the Physical Link 1.

Other more advanced concepts are also available if needed: Mission, Mode and State, Exchange Item, Class, Interface, etc. We shall discuss some of these in the context of the case study presented later in this work (Chapter 6).

1.2.6. *EPBS*

This level aims to deduce, from the Physical Architecture, the conditions that each Component must satisfy to comply with the constraints and choice of design of the architecture identified in the previous phases ("what is expected from the provider of each component"). The Physical Components are often grouped into larger Configuration Items that are easier to manage in terms of industrial organization and responsibilities.

The number of concepts proposed by Arcadia at this level is much smaller than for other levels. This is due to the fact that the main concept of this level is the Configuration Item, which can be divided into:

– System CI: system-type configuration item;

– Prime Item CI: decomposable configuration item;

– CSCI: computer software configuration item;

– HWCI: hardware configuration item;

– NDI: non-developed configuration item;

– COTS: *component off the shelf.*

In Figure 1.7, we can see four Configuration Items (gray rectangles). The first one, CSCI 1, is a software Configuration Item, carrying out Behavior Component 1. The second item, HWCI 2, is a material Configuration Item, carrying out Node Component 1, as well as Physical Link 1. The third, COTSCI 3, is an off the shelf Configuration Item, carrying out both Node Component 2 as well as Behavior Component 3. Finally, the fourth, NDICI 4 is a non-developed Configuration Item, carrying out Behavior Component 2.

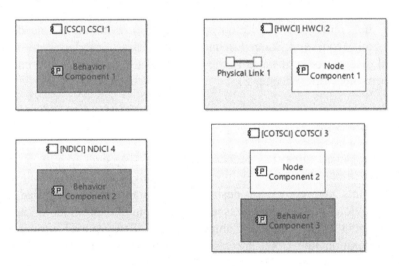

Figure 1.7. *Diagram showing the main concepts behind EPBS. For a color version of the figure, see www.iste.co.uk/roques/arcadia.zip*

1.3. Main types of Arcadia diagrams

This section provides an overview of the main types of diagrams defined by Arcadia and supported by Capella. This is not an exhaustive list of all of the diagrams available for each level of engineering, but rather a characterization of the different diagrams proposed.

1.3.1. *Data Flow diagrams*

The Data Flow diagrams are available at all levels in Arcadia. They represent the information dependency network between Functions. These diagrams provide a diverse set of mechanisms for managing complexity: simplified links calculated between the high-level Functions, the categorization of Exchanges, etc. The Functional Chains can be represented as highlighted paths.

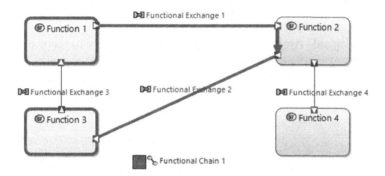

Figure 1.8. *Simple example of a Data flow diagram at the System level (SDFB), with a Functional Chain. For a color version of the figure, see www.iste.co.uk/roques/arcadia.zip*

1.3.2. *Architecture diagrams*

Architecture diagrams are used in all phases of engineering in Arcadia. Their main goal is to show the allocation of Functions to Components.

Functional Chains can be shown as highlighted paths. In System Analysis, these diagrams contain a box that represents the System under study and the Actors surrounding it.

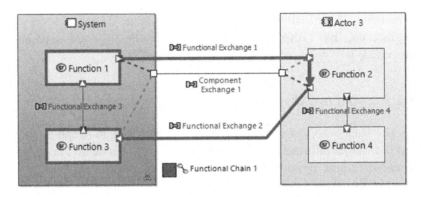

Figure 1.9. *Simple example of an Architecture diagram at the System level (SAB), with a Functional Chain. For a color version of the figure, see www.iste.co.uk/roques/arcadia.zip*

In Logical Architecture, these diagrams show the constitutive elements of the System. These are called Logical Components.

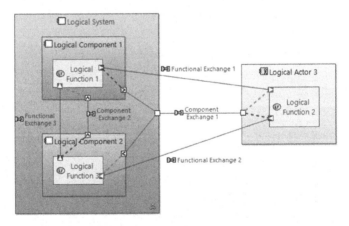

Figure 1.10. *Simple example of an Architecture diagram at the Logical level (LAB). For a color version of the figure, see www.iste.co.uk/roques/arcadia.zip*

In Physical Architecture, these diagrams also show the deployment of Behavior Components over the Node Components that provide them with resources.

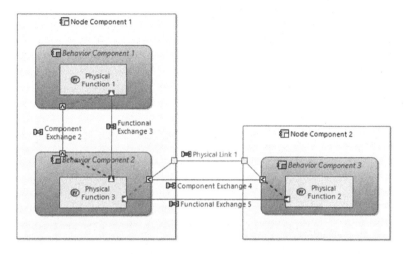

Figure 1.11. *Simple example of an Architecture diagram at the Physical level (PAB). For a color version of the figure, see www.iste.co.uk/roques/arcadia.zip*

1.3.3. *Scenario diagrams*

Scenario diagrams show the vertical sequence of the messages passed between elements (lifelines) and are largely inspired by the UML/SysML sequence diagram.

A lifeline (Instance Role, in Capella) is the representation of the existence of a model element that participates in the scenario involved. It has a name that reflects the name of the model element referenced and is represented graphically by a dotted vertical line. A Message is a unidirectional communication item between lifelines that triggers a behavior in the receiver.

Capella provides several types of Scenario diagrams: Functional Scenarios (the lifelines are Functions), Exchange Scenarios (the lifelines are Components/Actors, while the sequence Messages are Functional Exchanges or Component Exchanges), Interface Scenarios (the lifelines are Components/Actors, while the sequence Messages are Exchange Items). Modes, States and Functions can also be shown in these diagrams.

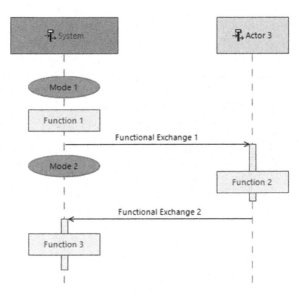

Figure 1.12. *Simple example of a diagram for*
an Exchange Scenario at the System level (SES)

A Scenario can call upon "subscenarios", defined elsewhere through a reference inserted between successive Exchanges along the time axis.

NOTE.– For more information on this type of diagram, the reader can refer to the following work: *Modélisation de systèmes complexes avec SysML* [CAS 18].

1.3.4. *Mode and State diagrams*

Mode and State diagrams are graphical representations of state machines inspired by UML/SysML. A state machine is a set of States linked together by Transitions. A Transition describes the reaction of a structural item when an event takes place (usually the item changes its State, but not always). A Transition contains a source State, a Trigger and a target State. It can also include a Guard Condition and an Effect.

NOTE.– Modes and States cannot exist together in the same machine. A Mode is an expected behavior, in the context of certain chosen conditions, of the System or of one of its Components, or of an Actor or an Operational Entity. A State is a behavior that is experienced by the System or one of its Components, or by an Actor or an Operational Entity, under certain conditions that are imposed by the environment. The term "State" will be used to the end of this section.

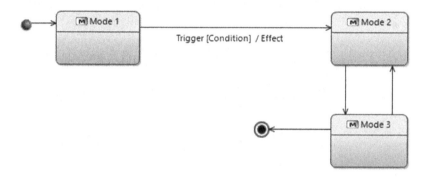

Figure 1.13. *Simple example of a Mode and State diagram (MSM)*

On top of the succession of "normal" States that correspond to the life cycle of a structural element, the diagram also shows two pseudo-states:

– the Initial State of the diagram corresponds to the creation of the structural element;

– the Final State of the diagram corresponds to the destruction of the structural element.

Modes/States/Transitions can be linked to Functions, Functional Exchanges, Exchange Items, etc.

NOTE.– For more information on this type of diagram, the reader can refer to the following work: *Modélisation de systèmes complexes avec SysML* [CAS 18].

1.3.5. *Breakdown diagrams*

Breakdown diagrams represent hierarchies of either Functions or Components at all levels of engineering.

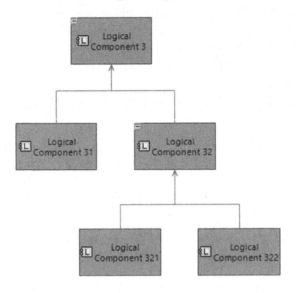

Figure 1.14. *Simple example of Component decomposition diagram at the Logical level (LCBD)*

1.3.6. *Class diagrams*

Capella provides advanced mechanisms for modeling data structures at a stated level of precision and for linking them to Functional Exchanges, Component or Function Ports, Interfaces, etc.

The Capella Class diagram draws heavily on the UML class diagram. Many of the same UML concepts are present: *Class, Enumeration, Type, Property, Association, Aggregation, Composition, Generalization, Package*, etc. More specific concepts are also present, however, in order to model the communication model, notably the Exchange Items.

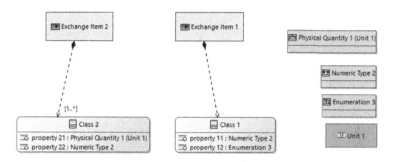

Figure 1.15. *Simple example of a Class diagram (CDB)*

NOTE.– For information on this type of diagram, the reader can refer to the following work: *UML 2 par la pratique – Études de cas et exercices corrigés* [ROQ 04].

1.3.7. *Capability diagrams*

Capability diagrams are available at every engineering phase in Arcadia, but are particularly useful in Operational Analysis and System Analysis. They can highlight the relations between Missions, Capabilities and Actors.

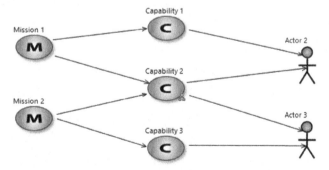

Figure 1.16. *Simple example of a Capability diagram at the System level (SMCB)*

We shall use all of these diagram types at least once in the following chapters as we go through the case study.

2

Capella: A System Modeling Solution

2.1. Radius considered and stakes involved

The goal of Arcadia is to contribute to the transformation of engineering by providing an engineering environment that offers a model-based procedure, rather than one based on documents, driven by a process, and which delivers effective coengineering by construction. To this end, the operational engineering experts at Thales have defined a unified language for modeling architectures in the group and have developed the associated toolbox, Capella, since 2007.

Unlike most companies that have tried to apply model based systems engineering (MBSE), Thales did not start by choosing a tool, for example *Rational Rhapsody (IBM)*, *MagicDraw (NoMagic)* or *Enterprise Architect (Sparx Systems)*, etc., with a language like systems modeling language (SysML). Experience shows that in such cases the system engineers have difficulties in getting started, as they lack both a methodological approach, which is not provided by SysML [VOI 16], and support tools. It is only during a later phase – if in the meantime the projects have not given up on modeling – that an approach adapted to the context can be developed. Even then, a toolbox still needs to be created, starting off with the commercial tool, which is often the source of unplanned extra costs....

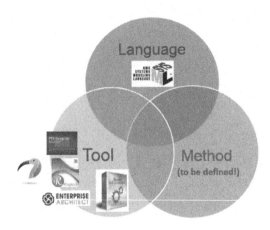

Figure 2.1. *"Classic" MBSE with SysML*

Thales started by defining a modeling method in order to improve its engineering practices: Arcadia. This method, which is based on functional analysis familiar to all system engineers, and on the allocation of functions to architecture components, implicitly defines a modeling language. As a result, the associated tool, Capella, knows both the language and the method, without requiring any extra thought or development.

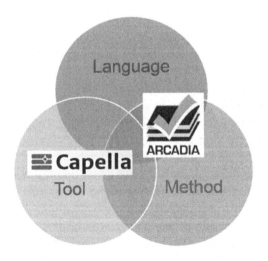

Figure 2.2. *MBSE with Arcadia/Capella*

Capella proposes similar ergonomics to tools like PowerPoint/Visio and Excel. As a result, the resulting environment is intuitive and allows engineers to concentrate on defining their architectures, rather than spending time learning and exploiting complex generic modeling languages such as UML or SysML in order to specify their needs. As it is dedicated to the underlying Arcadia method, Capella also guides engineers through their activities, something that generic modeling tools do not offer.

In 2015, the solution was provided as Open Source within the industry working-group PolarSys of the Eclipse Foundation, as part of the French collaborative Clarity project (www.clarity-se.org/), supported by BPI France. As a result, users of Capella benefit from 10 years of concrete feedback regarding the use of the Arcadia method and the associated tool (Melody Advance internally) with Thales projects.

Figure 2.3. *Welcome page of the Clarity project Website*

Capella has its own life cycle. A major version, providing new functionalities, is released at the end of each year, while several "minor" versions, providing patches for bugs, are released throughout the year. The download page can be found at www.polarsys.org/capella/download.html.

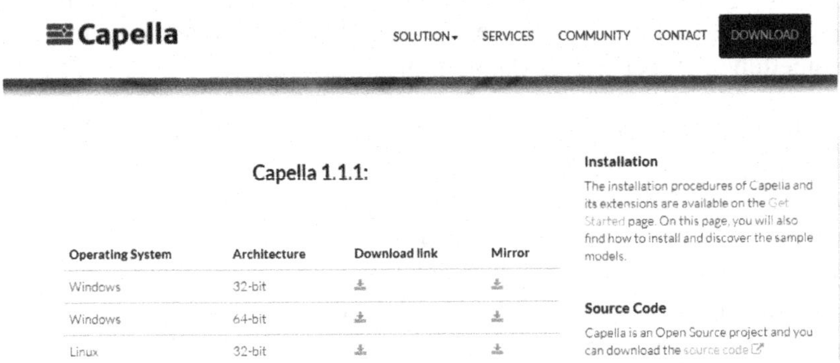

≡ Capella

SOLUTION ▾   SERVICES   COMMUNITY   CONTACT   DOWNLOAD

Capella 1.1.1:

Installation

The installation procedures of Capella and its extensions are available on the Get Started page. On this page, you will also find how to install and discover the sample models.

Operating System	Architecture	Download link	Mirror
Windows	32-bit	⬇	⬇
Windows	64-bit	⬇	⬇
Linux	32-bit	⬇	⬇

Source Code

Capella is an Open Source project and you can download the source code ⬀

Figure 2.4. *Download page of the Capella Website*

2.2. Principles of the tool

2.2.1. *Principles of the man–machine interface*

At the opening or creation of a Capella project, the interface of the tool is presented to the user. This contains different predefined zones (shown in the following), which we shall use many times during the case study in the following chapters. However, the user can modify the organization of the windows according to their preferences, by sliding/moving zones, hiding some of the views, or by showing others (command *Window – Show View –* etc.).

– The "Activity Browser" area exposes the user to the different engineering phases used in the modeling of their architecture, with shortcuts to create new diagrams linking to the engineering phase in question; this view also facilitates the "transition" between engineering phases in order to create realization links between the phases and their associated items.

– The "Semantic Browser" area allows the user to browse through the model with ease: for any item selected in the "project" area or on any diagram, the semantic browser area presents the user with all of the references that surround this item, i.e. its containment or reference relations, as well as all of the diagrams in which the element appears.

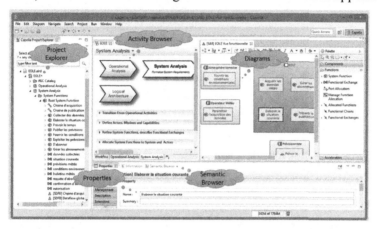

Figure 2.5. *Overview of the Capella interface. For a color version of the figure, see www.iste.co.uk/roques/arcadia.zip*

– The more typical "Project Explorer" area is a tree diagram of the Capella model, and contains all of the semantic items and diagrams created by the user.

– The "Diagram" area presents a graphical view of an extract of the model and allows the model to be edited in terms of creation, modifications, item deletion, as well as modifications to the organization or appearance of items in the diagram. The palette shown on the right depends on the type of diagram involved.

– The "Properties" zone, which shows all of the given properties for a selected item in the model or in a diagram.

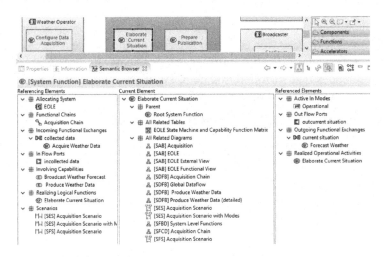

Figure 2.6. *Window of the Semantic Browser*

2.2.2. *Model element versus graphical object*

A key difference between a drawing tool, like Powerpoint or Visio, and a modeling tool lies in the coexistence of (but strong distinction between) graphical objects and model elements.

A Capella diagram contains a set of graphical objects that can be moved, resized, deleted, etc. Examples of graphical objects are the green rectangles of Functions, the blue rectangles of Components, the lines of Functional or Component Exchanges, etc. However, each graphical object in a Capella diagram is actually the visual representation of a model element. It is these model elements that carry the semantic information: name, type, etc. Most importantly, a single model element can be represented by different graphical objects in different diagrams.

In the example below, in the project explorer on the left we have shown a Logical Component called "Airborne Subsystem". This unique modeling element is represented on the right in three different diagrams:

– an Architecture diagram (LAB) where it is shown with an allocated Function (green rectangle inside);

– a Scenario diagram (LES) where it is shown as a vertical line exchanging Messages (horizontal arrows) with other Components or Logical Actors;

– a Breakdown diagram (LCBD) where it is shown alone, as it does not contain any Logical subcomponents.

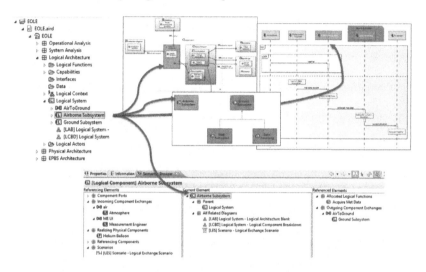

Figure 2.7. *Distinction between model element and graphical object (example). For a color version of the figure, see www.iste.co.uk/roques/arcadia.zip*

The "Airborne Subsystem" modeling element is also represented at the bottom of the *Semantic Browser*, where it is shown at the center, while all of the other elements linked to it are shown in the left and right columns. The three diagrams in which it is shown graphically are marked in the center column.

A slightly more sophisticated way of representing this distinction between model elements and graphical objects is provided in Figure 2.8, also produced using Capella *(Class Diagram Blank)*.

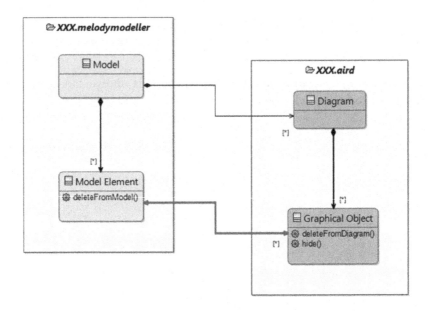

Figure 2.8. *Distinction between model element
and graphical object (concepts). For a color version
of the figure, see www.iste.co.uk/roques/arcadia.zip*

By default, a Capella model is stored in two files. As a simplification, the ".melodymodeller" can be said to contain the model elements and their relations, while the ".aird" contains the diagrams and the graphical objects. The fundamental point is represented by the red double arrow that links the model elements on the left with the graphical objects on the right.

A model element can be linked to none or several graphical objects. It is possible to create a model element without going through a diagram, and therefore without any graphical representation. This is quite rare, but permissible if there is no need for graphical communication around this element.

A graphical object is itself always linked to a single model element. There is one exception to this rule: graphical notes (in the form of little yellow "post-its"), which can be placed on any diagram as a purely graphical comment.

NOTE.– Selecting a graphical object in a diagram and pressing the *F8* key (or right clicking: *Show in Capella Explorer*) results in the model element being shown in the *Project Explorer*.

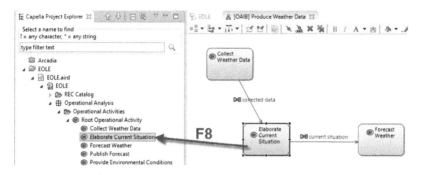

Figure 2.9. *From graphical object to model element (F8)*

It is very important to properly understand the two possible types of deletion:

– deletion of a graphical object (*Delete from Diagram*): command that is applied to a graphical object in the diagram, and therefore does not modify the model itself. The dependent graphical objects (links, ports, etc.) are also deleted. Note that even if the last graphical representation of a model element is destroyed, it continues to exist and can be reinserted into a diagram later on;

– deletion of a model element (*Delete from Model*): command applied to a graphical object in a diagram, or on a model element in the project explorer that is applied to the model element involved. This command changes the model itself and can lead to a cascade of deletions, as the deletion of a Function automatically leads to the deletion of the ingoing and outgoing Functional Exchanges, its Ports, its allocation relation with structural items, etc. All linked graphical objects are also deleted from all of the diagrams involved.

The importance of the deletion of a model element is signaled by Capella in the form of a window that pops up to show which other model elements would also be permanently erased.

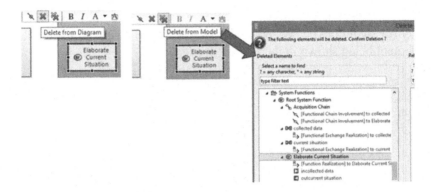

Figure 2.10. *Distinction between the deletion of a model element and a graphical object*

A graphical object can also be hidden (*Hide element*), rather than completely deleted from the diagram. The difference with deletion is subtle: the graphical object is still present, but no longer visible. The dependent graphical objects (links, ports, etc.) are also hidden. There is a *Show/Hide* button in the palette at the top of the diagram.

NOTE.– Do not overuse the *"Hide"* feature: the graphical object still exists and weighs down the ".aird" file. Its use must be punctual, for example to temporarily mask an object without losing the graphical work (position, size, etc.), before bringing it back to the diagram.

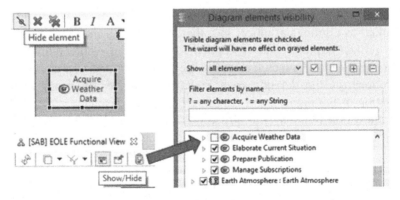

Figure 2.11. *Distinction between hiding and deleting a graphical object*

2.2.3. *Integrated methodological guidance*

Capella has an integrated methodological guide in the form of the *Activity Explorer*. This lists the various activities and the different diagrams that can be carried out at the relevant level of engineering, for example in this case System Analysis. Figure 2.12 first shows the activities, and then each activity shows the relevant diagrams.

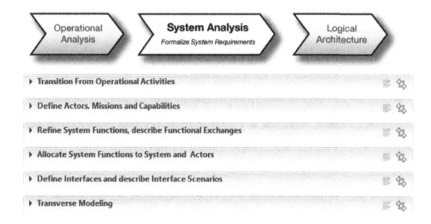

Figure 2.12. *Methodological activities of the "System Analysis" level*

For example, if we open the *Refine System Functions* activity, Capella proposes three types of diagram:

– a Functional Breakdown diagram (SFBD), which allows for the creation of Functions and subfunctions;

– a Data Flow diagram (SDFB), which allows for the creation of Functions and subfunctions, and for them to be linked through Functional Exchanges;

– a Functional Scenario diagram (FS), which also allows for the creation of Functions and Functional Exchanges.

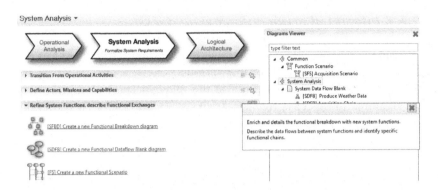

Figure 2.13. *Methodological activity in detail*

Capella offers the possibility of filtering the diagrams in the *"Diagrams Viewer"* against a single methodological activity in order to reduce the number of visible diagrams. For example, here we can filter over the chosen activity, and thus only see the *SFBD, SDFB* or *FS* diagrams.

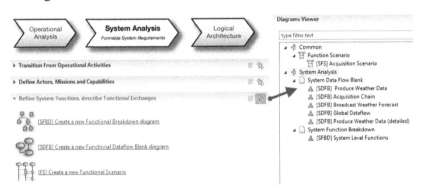

Figure 2.14. *Filtering of the diagrams by methodological activity*

It must be noted that the tool provides a rather complete online help section, which can be accessed via the *Help–Help Contents* menu. The window that opens provides a large amount of information; what interests us here is the *Capella Guide*, which contains the *Release Note*, the *User Manual*, but also a *Developer Manual* (for

Capella Studio), a list of diagrams and validation rules, as well as a glossary.

Figure 2.15. *Capella online help*

NOTE.– If the *Activity Explorer* is closed accidentally, it can always be opened again by right clicking on the .aird in the *Project Explorer*.

2.2.4. Different natures of diagrams

At each engineering level in Arcadia, Capella proposes a large number of very similar diagrams. In section 1.3, we mentioned the main types of diagram in terms of methodology. Another classification can be made from the tool point of view. The management rules of the different natures of the diagrams, especially in the case of a model element being added, are characterized by precise rules that we shall describe below.

We shall first distinguish the three natures of the most frequent diagrams in Capella, using their specific denomination:

– Breakdown *(xxBD)*;

– Blank *(xxB)*;

– Scenario *(xxS)*.

The *Breakdown* diagrams (written *xxBD*) represent tree diagrams of either functions or components, at all levels of engineering. We can name for example:

– the Operational level: OABD (activities), OEBD (entities);

– the System level: SFBD (functions);

– the Logical level: LFBD (functions), LCBD (components);

– the Physical level: PFBD (functions), PCBD (components);

– the EPBS level: CIBD (configuration items).

NOTE.– These diagrams always represent the current state of the model and are updated automatically by default. As soon as a *Breakdown* type diagram element model is created, whether by another type of diagram or by the explorer, the *Breakdown* is updated automatically. *Breakdown* diagrams are designed to be complete, even though some elements can be hidden (*Hide element*) in order to simplify it. However, the command *Delete from Diagram* is switched off by default, as the diagram is automatically updated the next time it is opened....

Blank diagrams, written *xxB*, are usually the most common in a Capella model. They exist at all levels of engineering. We can name for example:

– the Operational level: OAIB (activities and interactions), OCB (capabilities), OAB (architecture), ORB (roles), CDB (classes);

– the System level: SDFB (functions), CB/MCB (missions and capabilities), SAB (architecture), CDB (classes);

– the Logical level: LDFB (functions), LAB (architecture), CDB (classes);

– the Physical level: PDFB (functions), PAB (architecture), CDB (classes);

– the EPBS level: EAB (architecture).

NOTE.– Unlike the previous ones, these diagrams are not meant to be comprehensive and are not automatically updated. They are empty on creation, hence the name *Blank*, even if model elements of a compatible type already exist. It is the modeler who decides which subset of compatible model elements they are going to represent graphically, as a function of who is reading the diagram, and what their objectives are.

As a result, in this type of diagram the modeler can either:

– create a graphical object by also creating a model element (thus modifying the model);

– insert an existing model element into the diagram so as to only create a new graphical object (therefore without modifying the model).

The distinction between these two choices can be seen systematically in the palettes of the *Blank* diagrams, as shown in Figure 2.16.

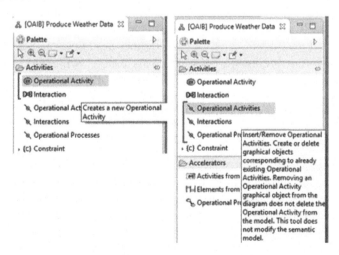

Figure 2.16. *Creation or insertion of model elements in a Blank*

NOTE.– When a *compatible model element* is created, whether by another diagram or by the explorer, the *Blank* diagram is not updated automatically. However, the links between elements, such as Functional Exchanges, etc., only appear automatically if the source and the target of the links are already present on the diagram. These management rules had been tested and approved by Thales projects as being the most effective long before Capella was made available as Open Source.

The *Scenario* diagrams (written *xxS*) are also present for all engineering levels. We can name for example:

– Operational level: OAS (activities), OES (entities);

– System level: SFS (functions), SES (exchanges), SIS (interfaces);

– Logical level: LFS (functions), LES (exchanges), LIS (interfaces);

– Physical level: PFS (functions), PES (exchanges), PIS (interfaces);

– EPBS level: EIS (interfaces).

The Scenario diagram in Capella is very close to the UML/SysML sequence diagram [CAS 18]. It shows a vertical sequence of Messages passed from model element to model element (called *lifeline* in UML/SysML). However, Capella provides several types of Scenario diagrams: Functional Scenarios (the lifelines are Functions), Exchange Scenarios (the lifelines are Components/Actors while the sequence Messages are Functional or Component Exchanges), Interface Scenarios (the lifelines are Components/Actors while the sequence Messages are Exchange Items).

NOTE.– It must noted that the model elements that appear in a Scenario diagram are references to other model elements. For example, the vertical lines of Actors and the horizontal Messages in the Exchange Scenarios refer, respectively, to the Actors and to the Functional Exchanges of the model. By selecting a graphical object in a Scenario diagram and by pressing *F8* (or right clicking: *Show in Capella Explorer*), we get the model element contained in the Scenario represented in the *Project Explorer*. By instead pressing *F7*, we get the referenced model element.

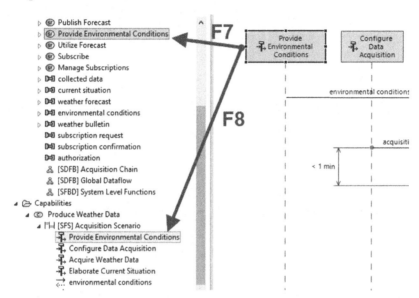

Figure 2.17. *Model elements referenced in a Scenario*

As a result, deletion is a bit more complex: note that the model element deleted by the *Delete from Model* is the same as the one contained in the scenario, and not the one referenced. Moreover, if the referenced element is deleted, the choice that has been made involves displaying a graphical element in the scenario that no longer points to any model element, showing an error that needs to be corrected. It would be very dangerous to also destroy all the elements in the scenarios by cascade, following the deletion of an actor or of a function, as the modeler would have no simple way to detect the scenario changes.

In the example from Figure 2.17, by deciding to delete the Function and not only the vertical line in the Scenario, we would obtain an updated diagram with *Invalid feature as name* and *undefined* indications for the orphan graphical objects. A model validation would invariably result in associated errors.

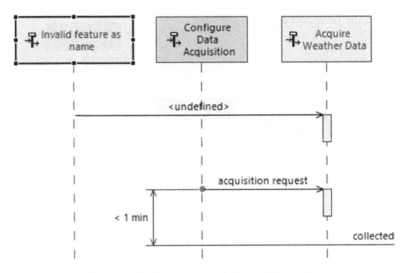

Figure 2.18. *Orphan elements in a Scenario*

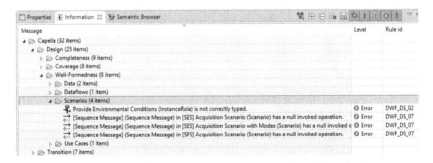

Figure 2.19. *Errors linked to orphan elements in a scenario*

NOTE.– The Scenario diagram is the only one that does not allow a *Delete from Diagram* or a *Hide Element* to be carried out on the vertical lines or on the horizontal messages. This is a very particular diagram, since the model elements being handled are local to the Scenario in question and are only represented by a single graphical object.

2.2.5. *Additional information on the diagrams*

In the previous section, we discussed the management rules involved in the different natures of diagrams, particularly in the case of a model element being added.

For example, we explained that *Breakdown* diagrams are automatically updated, as soon as a relevant model element is created, whether by another type of diagram or by the explorer. We have also explained that in *Blank* type diagrams, the links between elements such as Functional Exchanges etc. only appear automatically if the source and the target of the links are already present on the diagram.

There is an advanced method for voluntarily blocking these automatic updates. This can be in the interest of performance levels in very large models, or simply to more precisely control what appears in each diagram. By default, the diagrams are said to be synchronized, but they can be desynchronized in order to update them when and how the modeler desires. This is done by ticking a property of the diagram called *Unsynchronized* by right clicking at the back of the diagram.

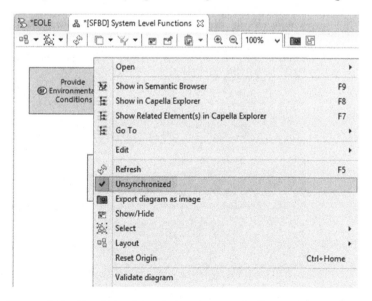

Figure 2.20. *Example of desynchronization of a Breakdown diagram*

In the previous example of a Function Breakdown diagram at the System level (*SFBD*), we can now see that the command *Delete from Diagram* is active, contrary to what we had previously explained for Breakdown diagrams. Most importantly, if a Function is added to a *Data Flow* diagram (*SDFB*), this function will not automatically appear in the *SFBD*.

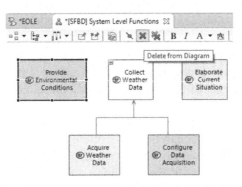

Figure 2.21. *Modification of the available commands following desynchronization of a Breakdown diagram*

In the same way, if we place the *Unsynchronized* property on a *Blank* diagram, the links do not appear automatically.

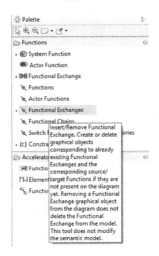

Figure 2.22. *Command for inserting functional exchanges*

In this way, we can choose whether to insert them or not based on the objectives of each individual diagram.

NOTE.– By default, use of the command *Insert/Remove Functional Exchanges* in a *Blank* diagram does not make sense. It only becomes useful once the diagram has been desynchronized. In the same way, the *Delete from Diagram* command is only active for the links (Functional Exchanges, etc.) if the diagram has been desynchronized.

We must also add the possibility of "cloning" a diagram, for example to derive a simplified view from it by deleting certain graphical objects, or by masking certain element types using filters predefined by Capella. We will make use of this command several times during the case study.

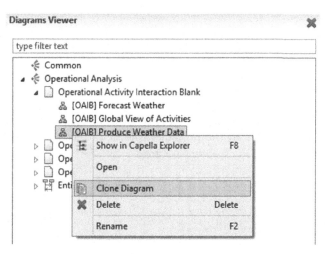

Figure 2.23. *Diagram cloning command*

Another very useful concept for dealing with the complexity of the diagrams is that of Category. Starting with a set of Functional Exchanges, Component Exchanges or Physical Links, a new model element can be created that allows for a graphical synthesis of the multiple links to take place. This concept is available at the System Analysis level, as well as at the Logical and Physical Architecture levels.

Let us look at the simple example of two System Functions with multiple Functional Exchanges, such as in Figure 2.24. Here, we can ask for the creation of a Category in order to carry out the synthesis.

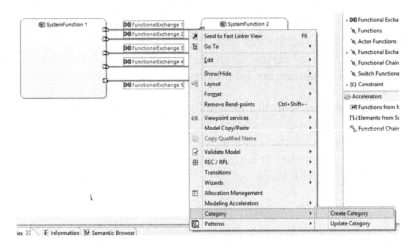

Figure 2.24. *Contextual Category creation command*

The category *ExchangeCategory 1* thus created is a new model element that appears in the project explorer at the same level as the technical element *Root System Function*.

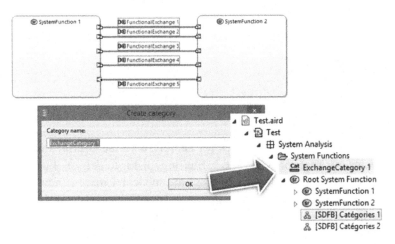

Figure 2.25. *Result of Category creation*

It is then possible to request to visualize the Category instead of the set of links that it represents, thus simplifying the diagram in question. This is done through the *Switch Functional Exchanges/Categories* command in the palette.

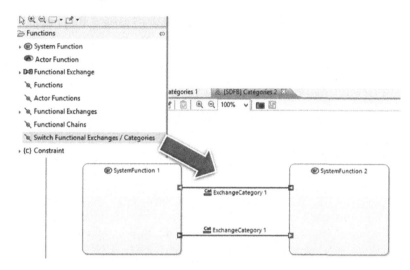

Figure 2.26. *On demand Category display*

The concept of Category is particularly useful at the level of Physical Architecture in order to synthesize the multiple Physical Links between two Node Components, connecting pins between electrical components for example.

2.2.6. *Embedded requirements management solution*

In the same way that the SysML language [CAS 18] integrates the concept of *Requirement* in order to improve traceability between requirements and design elements or test cases, Capella proposes a simple embedded solution for managing requirements.

The goal here is obviously not to completely replace a requirement management tool such as IBM *Doors* (https://en.wikipedia.org/wiki/Rational_DOORS), but rather to propose a simple and integrated alternative for defining requirements that allows them to later be linked to any model element: Function, Functional Chain, Capability, etc.

In Capella, first a specific package must be created in the *Project Explorer* called *Requirements Pkg* in order to create Requirements later.

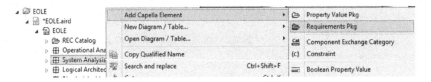

Figure 2.27. *Requirements package creation command*

It is then possible to create *Requirement*-type model elements. Capella proposes a certain number of predefined variations: *Functional Requirement, Non-Functional Requirement*, etc.

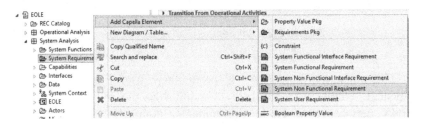

Figure 2.28. *Requirement creation command*

A Requirement created in this way possesses a relatively complete and specific property sheet, allowing the verification method or the unique requirement identifier to be specified, for instance. In our example, we shall create a Requirement at the System level in terms of the performance of meteorological data acquisition.

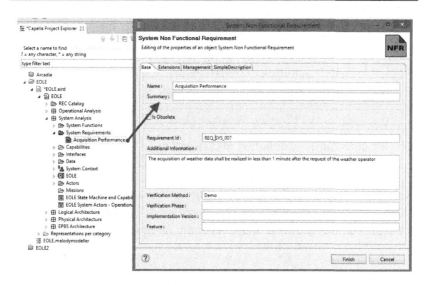

Figure 2.29. *Property sheet of a Requirement*

A Capella Requirement can then be linked to either any other model Requirement (*Requirement Manager*), or to any model element (*Trace Manager*), at any level of Arcadia. This is therefore a very flexible embedded traceability management solution.

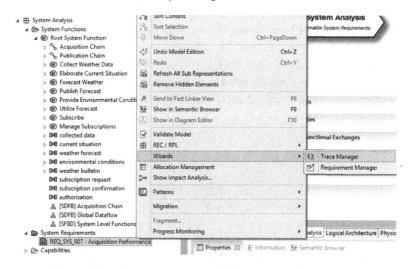

Figure 2.30. *Contextual menu for Requirement traceability*

In our case study, we might want to link this performance requirement to:

– the Function "Acquire Weather Data";

– the Functional Chain "Acquisition Chain";

– the Capability "Produce Weather Data";

– the constraint *"acquisition max duration"*.

All of these model elements are discussed in Chapter 4. As an example, let us link the Requirement to the acquisition Functional Chain. The link created by the contextual menu *Wizards–Trace Manager* can then be seen in the *Semantic Browser*.

Figure 2.31. *Generic traceability link in the Semantic Browser*

A more finalized solution of Requirements management is being developed and will be available in the near future as a specific *viewpoint* (a beta version is already available on the Capella Website). Notably, this tool will allow us to import a set of existing requirements from a specialized requirements management tool such as Doors, using the standardized format ReqIF.

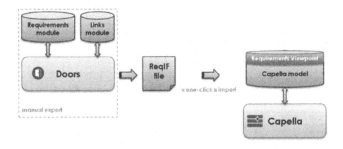

Figure 2.32. *Future Requirements viewpoint*

3

Complete Example of Modeling with Capella: Operational Analysis

3.1. Presentation of the case study and project creation

3.1.1. *Presentation of the EOLE case study*

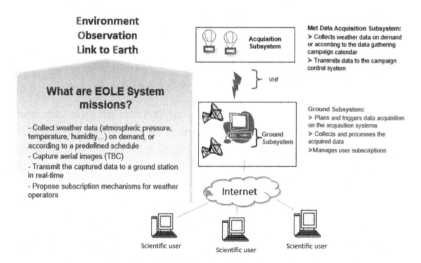

Figure 3.1. *Simplified specifications of the "EOLE" system*

The example used to illustrate the main aspects involved in putting Capella into practice is "EOLE", a sounding weather balloon system, whose main goal is to provide meteorological data for various scientific users.

Although simple, the EOLE system is, nonetheless, representative of the issues regarding systems engineering due to its:

– multiple stakeholders and user types;

– different types of components (hardware, software, etc.);

– different types of functional and non-functional requirements.

This same case study has been used since 2008 to illustrate the Thales University's own training programs, quickly thrusting the trainees into concrete situations.

It is also used in Capella training programs organized by PRFC (www.prfc.fr/formation/capella-in-action/). More than 120 training sessions have been successfully delivered, consolidating the pedagogical value of the "EOLE" case study over the years.

The reader can obtain more information on the subject on Wikipedia: en.wikipedia.org/wiki/Weather_balloon.

NOTE.– The purpose of this book is not to provide an ideal "correction" for this case study in terms of its execution, but rather to illustrate the main possible uses of the Capella tool and the underlying Arcadia method. The modeling process that we shall go through together is therefore strongly influenced by this teaching objective. Do not forget that a good model is a model that provides satisfactory answers to predefined questions.

3.1.2. *Creation of the EOLE project*

Once Capella has been started, there are two ways to create a new project. The first involves using the *Welcome* window and clicking on *New Capella Project*.

Figure 3.2. Welcome *window on opening Capella*

The second way involves activating the same command by going through the *File* menu in the toolbar on top.

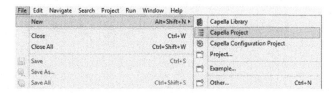

Figure 3.3. *Creation of a new project through the "File" menu*

The project must then be named, avoiding names already taken in the same workspace, and possibly changing the directory where it is stored (by unticking *Use default location*).

Figure 3.4. *First window in new project creation*

Then click on *Next* > to select the desired Arcadia levels.

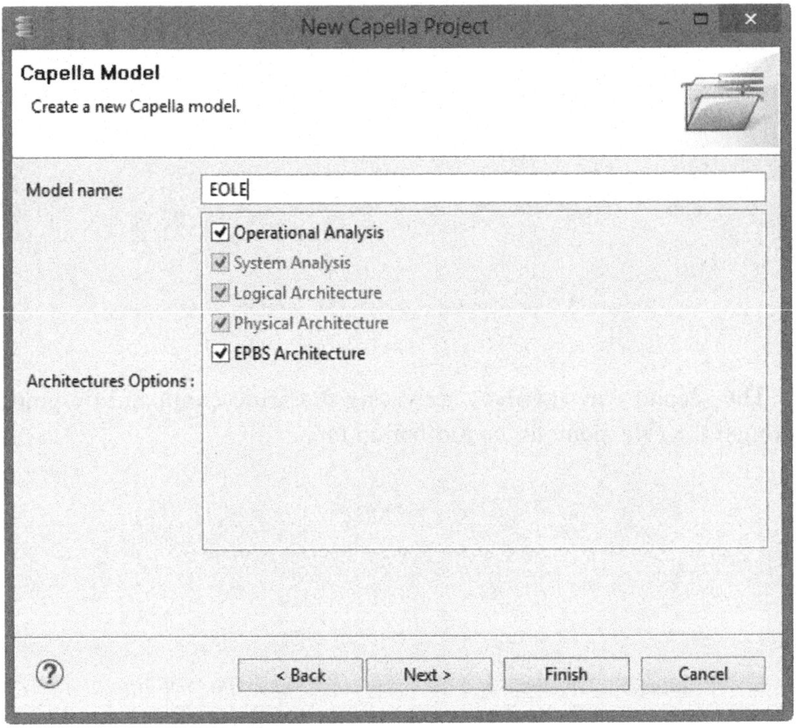

Figure 3.5. *Second window in new project creation*

All levels are selected by default. Only the first (Operational Analysis) and the last level (EPBS) are optional in the tool. This is because realization links can only be established between two successive levels. Click on *Finish* to finalize creation of the model.

NOTE.– Even if the Logical Architecture is optional in the Arcadia method, it is not with the Capella tool. To overcome this issue, the tool offers automatic transitions that allow the Logical level to be initialized from the System level in a few clicks.

The model obtained in this way contains a first level of folders that correspond to the selected engineering levels. Next, each level contains subfolders for their major concepts. For example, at the Operational Analysis level there are folders for Activities, Capabilities, Entities, etc.

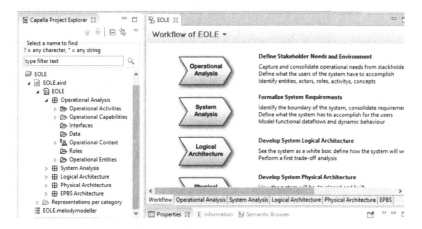

Figure 3.6. *Result of the creation of a new project*

The engineering levels and corresponding activities are also recalled in the main window where the diagrams are shown, with an *Activity Explorer* type diagram created automatically. In this case, it is called "Workflow of EOLE".

3.2. Operational Analysis

3.2.1. *Main concepts and diagrams*

Capella has an integrated methodological guide in the form of the *Activity Explorer*. This lists the various activities and the different diagrams that can be produced at the relevant engineering level, which in this case is Operational Analysis. Figures 3.7–3.9 first state these activities, and then the possible diagrams.

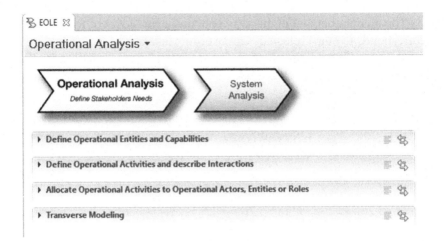

Figure 3.7. *Methodological activities of the "Operational Analysis" level*

We shall not discuss the Transverse Modeling group at this level, which contains the Mode and State diagrams, as well as the Class diagrams for data modeling. This methodological activity exists at each Arcadia level (except EPBS), hence the name of Transverse Modeling. We shall make the most of System Analysis to look at this further.

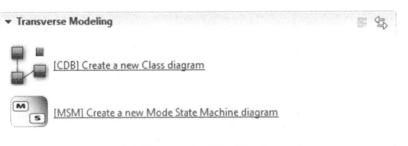

Figure 3.8. *"Transverse" Capella diagrams*

Figure 3.9. *Capella diagrams at the "Operational Analysis" level*

NOTE.– Although Arcadia is a method, the modeling process is completely flexible. The methodological activities presented in the *Activity Explorer* are nearly all optional and can be carried out in any order, and this is also the case for the diagrams.

We are therefore going to make an arbitrary but reasoned choice for the realization of diagrams at each level of engineering. Here, we shall start by defining high-level objectives, called Operational Capabilities. We shall provide details regarding these Capabilities through a network of Operational Activities that exchange Interactions. Next, we will complete the analysis by allocating the Activities to Operational Entities. Last, we shall discuss additional concepts, such as Operational Scenarios, Operational Processes, etc.

3.2.2. *Operational Capabilities and Entities*

Operational Analysis involves carrying out domain modeling, often called business modeling, independently of the future system to be realized. The idea is to voluntarily break from the system under study, by going back up a level, in order to return to the "real" needs of the various stakeholders.

How can this need be characterized synthetically in the domain of meteorology? We can start by identifying Operational Capabilities, for example: "Produce Meteorological Data" and "Forecast Weather", which has surely been the ultimate goal for millennia.

To do this, we create an OCB (Operational Capabilities Blank).

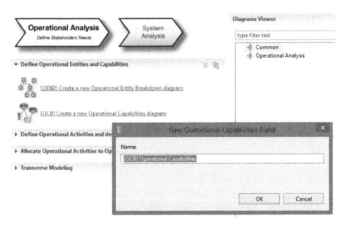

Figure 3.10. *Creation of an Operational Capability Blank (OCB) diagram*

The diagram created is empty by default (*Blank*). It allows not only for the creation of Operational Capabilities, but also of Operational Entities and Actors, and the numerous relations between them. Let us start with the two Operational Capabilities mentioned above. We can link them to entities/actors of the domain as they are discovered. For example, the Capability, "Forecast Weather" involves an Operational Actor "Forecaster"; "Produce Meteorological Data" involves a "Weather Operator". Note that for the moment the goal is not to be exhaustive, and we shall return to the diagram later.

NOTE.– The modeling process is intrinsically iterative and incremental. The different types of diagrams allow the subject to be tackled from other viewpoints: concepts discovered in one diagram allow others to be completed.

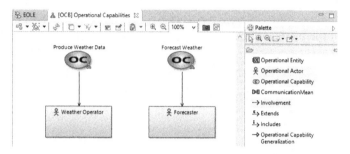

Figure 3.11. *First version of the Operational Capability Blank (OCB) diagram*

If we open the property sheet of an Operational Capability (OC), we see that it can be linked to other concepts such as Activities, Processes, Modes and States, etc. The *Involved Entities* field has automatically been filled in by Capella as a result of the relations (involvement) created in the diagram.

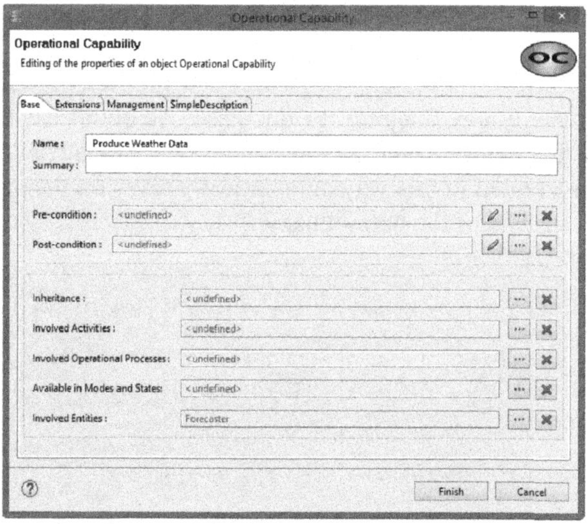

Figure 3.12. *Property sheet of an Operational Capability (OC)*

3.2.3. *Operational Activities and Interactions*

For each OC, we shall create a set of Activities linked together by Interactions. The type of diagram chosen is a Data Flow diagram between Activities, called OAIB (Operational Activity Interaction Blank). However, it is also possible to proceed in a different manner, for example by describing Operational Scenarios instead.

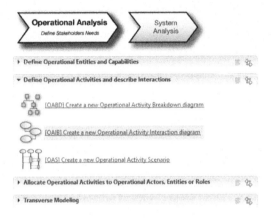

Figure 3.13. *Creation of a diagram showing Operational Activities and Interactions (OAIB)*

It is not always necessary to go through the *Activity Explorer* in order to create a new diagram. In this case, we could have created a contextual diagram by right clicking on an OC. The advantage is that the diagram created in this way automatically takes on the name of the Capability, instead of the default name.

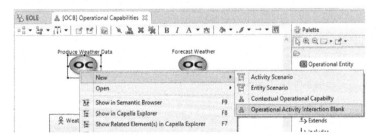

Figure 3.14. *Creation of an OAIB diagram through the contextual menu*

The diagram created is empty by default (*Blank*). It allows us to create Operational Activities, as well as the Interactions that link them.

We can thus create a first series of Activities, with inputs and outputs that link them, as in the figure below. This could be the result of a preliminary work meeting with experts in the domain, for example.

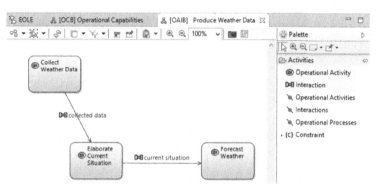

Figure 3.15. *First version of the contextual OAIB with the Capability "Produce Weather Data"*

NOTE.– An Interaction can only be shown on a diagram if its target and source Activities are present. This is why we have shown the Activity "Forecast Weather" in the first diagram, to show the output "current situation", even though this Activity is clearly the central Activity of the other OC. Let us not forget that one modeling element can easily appear in several diagrams.

We do the same for the second Capability by adding a new activity "Publish Forecast".

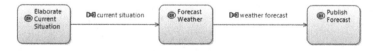

Figure 3.16. *Contextual OAIB with the Capability "Forecast Weather"*

It is then very easy to create a third OAIB, this time from the *Activity Explorer*, bringing together all of the Activities. These only need to be inserted into the empty diagram using the palette command *Insert/Remove Operational Activities* by pressing on the *Add all elements* button.

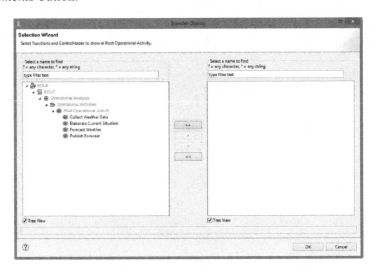

Figure 3.17. *Insertion of all Operational Activities in a global OAIB*

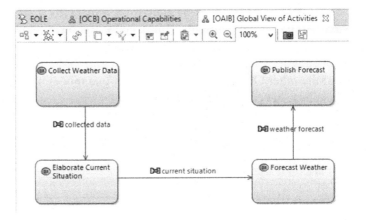

Figure 3.18. *Global OAIB obtained by insertion of all Operational Activities*

In order to visualize the diagrams in which each modeling element does or does not appear, the most efficient way is always to go via the *Semantic Browser*. If, for example, we select the Activity "Elaborate current situation", we can see that it is represented graphically in the three OAIB.

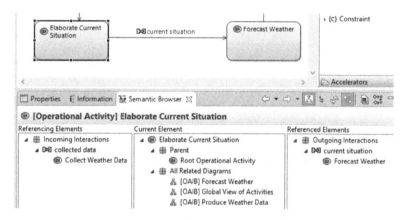

Figure 3.19. *Activity selection in the Semantic Browser*

3.2.4. *Allocation of Activities to the Operational Entities*

Capella offers a feature of methodological verification through its validation rules. A first opportunity to put this into practice is already available here: Activities (just like Functions at the lower levels) must be allocated to structural elements, which in Operational Analysis is to Operational Entities or Actors.

There are several verification methods available to us. We can ask for the complete validation of the model, of an engineering level or even of only a folder of the project explorer, by right clicking.

The results of the validation are then shown as requested by type in the *Information* window, located beside the *Semantic Browser* and below the diagrams, after clicking *OK* on the pop-up window of the *Validation Problems*. The rules folders must be opened progressively in order to show the results in detail.

Here, we will only look at the group called *Completeness*, which informs us that the four Activities are not allocated to any structural element.

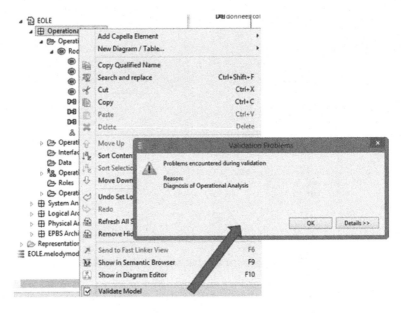

Figure 3.20. *Application of the command "Validate Model" in the Project Explorer at the Operational level*

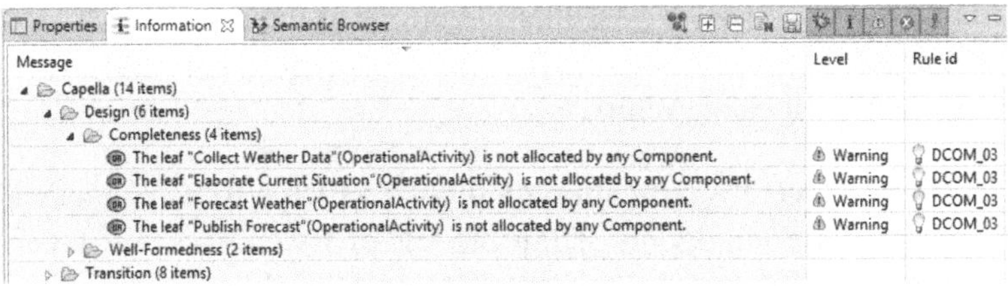

Figure 3.21. *Results from the validation of the Operational Activities*

All of the validation rules are accessible via the menu *Window – Preferences – Model Validation – Constraints – Capella*. These can be turned on or off one by one or by group.

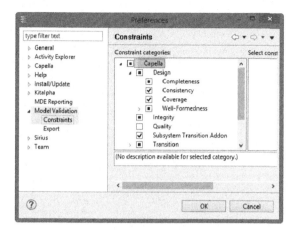

Figure 3.22. *Capella validation rules*

In order to allocate the Activities, we create a particular type of diagram, which is probably the most important type at each level of engineering: an Architecture Blank diagram (*xAB*). This is therefore here an Operational Architecture Blank (OAB).

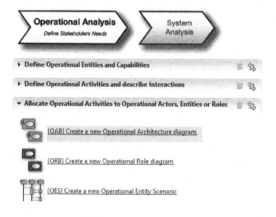

Figure 3.23. *Creation of an Operational Architecture Blank (OAB) diagram*

The diagram created is empty by default (*Blank*). It allows for both Operational Entities and/or Actors, as well as Activities, to be created, and for the allocation of Activities to Entities to be managed.

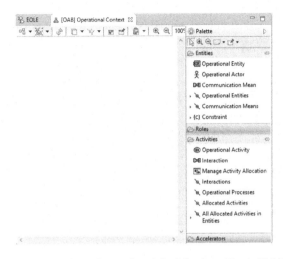

Figure 3.24. *Palette of the Operational Architecture Blank (OAB) diagram*

At each level of Arcadia, this is the type of diagram that offers the most complex palette. Even when hiding the *Roles* group (an advanced concept that we will not use) and the *Accelerators* group, there are many other commands left in the palette.

We first insert the Entities/Actors already created during the Operational Capabilities diagram. Next, we allocate to them the obvious Activities, using the *Manage Activity Allocation* button.

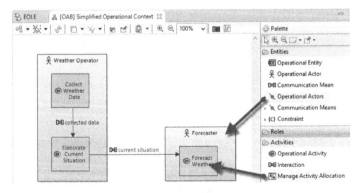

Figure 3.25. *Start of the Operational Architecture Blank (OAB) diagram. For a color version of the figure, see www.iste.co.uk/roques/arcadia.zip*

NOTE.– It is worth noting that existing Interactions only appear if the target and source Activities are already present in the diagram (and the *Unsynchronized* property has not been ticked).

We still need to allocate the activity "Publish Forecast", but to do this we need to create a new Operational Actor, the "Broadcaster", as this is a different job profile from the forecaster and the weather operator.

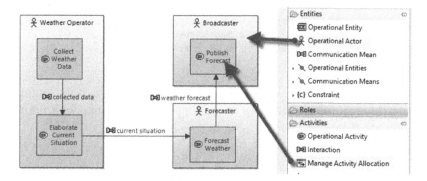

Figure 3.26. *Follow-on of the Operational Architecture Blank (OAB) diagram. For a color version of the figure, see www.iste.co.uk/roques/arcadia.zip*

Furthermore, we also want to show that these three profiles all belong to the same organization: "Weather Services Provider". To do this, we create an Operational Entity that can contain the three Actors. The containment relation is created by sliding them around in the rectangle of the Entity. We also add an Operational Actor that does not belong to the same organization, who will use the forecasts. To finish off, we can add a final Operational Entity that represents the Earth's atmosphere and which provides the environmental conditions.

NOTE.– The physical environment is often an important Actor at the System Analysis level, but should not be forgotten in Operational Analysis.

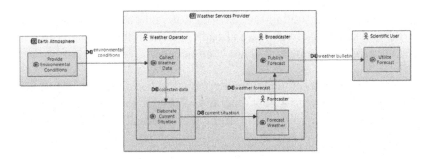

Figure 3.27. *Remainder and end of the Operational Architecture diagram (OAB). For a color version of the figure, see www.iste.co.uk/roques/arcadia.zip*

We can now make sure that the model validation is only issuing "transition warnings", relating to missing realization links with future elements of System level.

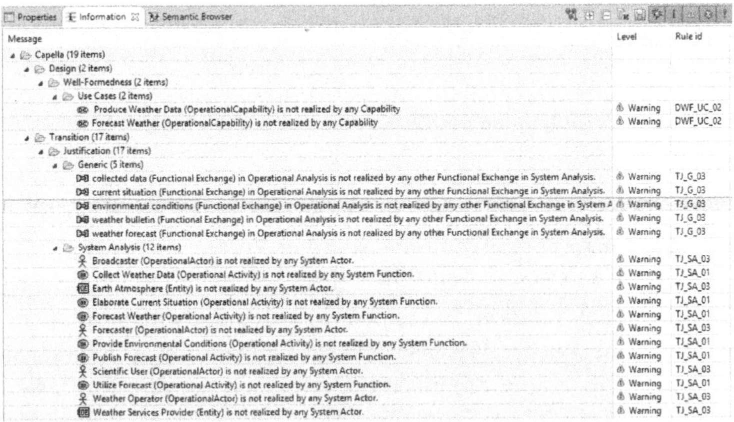

Figure 3.28. *Results from the validation of the Operational Analysis*

3.2.5. *Additional diagrams and concepts*

In this section, we shall introduce two new types of diagrams. First, a breakdown diagram, of which there can be two types in Operational Analysis: an Activity Breakdown diagram (*OABD*) or an Entity Breakdown diagram (*OEBD*).

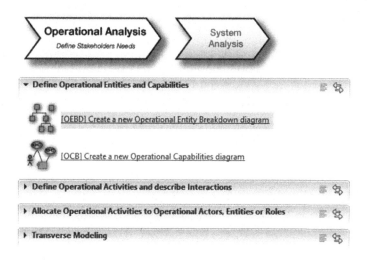

Figure 3.29. *Creation of an Entity Breakdown diagram (OEBD)*

For our case study, there was no need to break down the Activities into subactivities. However, we wanted to introduce an Operational Entity that tied together a number of Operational Actors, which is often the case when modeling an organization. As a result, if we ask Capella to produce the breakdown diagram of the entities (*OEBD* – Operational Entity Breakdown) after making our OAB, the *OEBD* is generated and updated automatically.

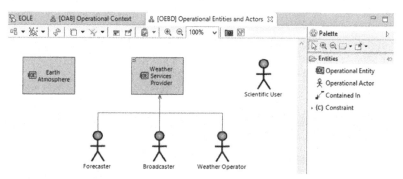

Figure 3.30. *Breakdown diagram of the Operational Entities (OEBD)*

The palettes of breakdown diagrams are the simplest in Capella. They only allow for the creation of one particular type of modeling element (with possible variation, such as Entity/Actor in this case) and only the containment relation.

The second type of diagram that we shall introduce is now called a Scenario. In Operational Analysis, there can be two types of Scenario diagram: diagrams with the Activities as vertical lines (*OAS*) or with the Entities or Actors (*OES*).

Figure 3.31. *The two types of diagram for Operational Scenarios*

In order to illustrate our understanding of the domain, let us take the example of an *OES*. This way, we can show the process represented in the Data Flow or Architecture diagrams, but focusing more on the chronological aspects.

NOTE.– A Scenario diagram is linked to a Scenario type model element in Capella, which is itself always tied to a Capability.

When we create an *OES*, Capella makes us choose to which Capability to link it. Let us choose the OC "Forecast Weather", for example. The Scenario diagram is very powerful and close to the UML/SysML sequence diagram. The palette therefore offers a very large number of possible commands.

We start by inserting Operational Actors we are interested in. We could also create new ones if any were missing.

Next, we choose the type of messages that are passed along the vertical lines. These can correspond to Interactions, which is the most intuitive, but they can also reference communication means, or *"timers"*, etc. We choose to use existing Interactions.

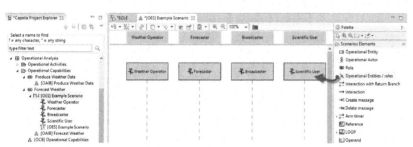

Figure 3.32. *Start of Scenario diagram (OES)*

We can also represent the execution of the Activities along the vertical lines to which they are allocated, using the command *Insert/Remove Activity* from the palette.

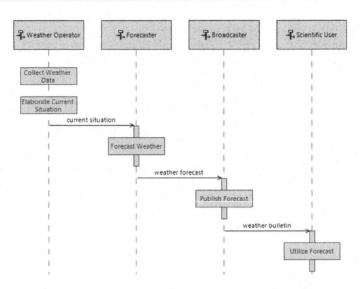

Figure 3.33. *Follow-on of the Scenario diagram (OES)*

In order to illustrate what can be expressed by the Scenario diagram, we can add a *LOOP Fragment*, which indicates that the process represented is repeated every day.

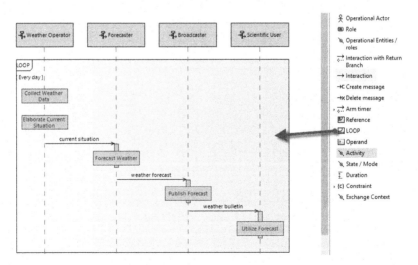

Figure 3.34. *Remainder and end of the Scenario diagram (OES). For a color version of the figure, see www.iste.co.uk/roques/arcadia.zip*

NOTE.– To edit the loop condition, first the Operand property sheet contained within it must be opened, and then we must go to the field called *Guard*. In the *Guard* field, the command represented by the crayon icon must be activated, called *Create a new element*. This opens a new window called *Opaque Expression*. The body of this expression is not edited in the *Name* field, but by clicking on *Linked Text*, and by typing text on the right. This is a general mechanism for entering constraints, which we shall see again later.

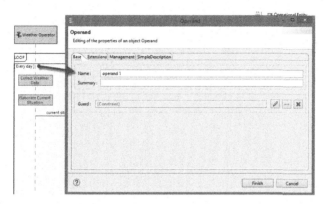

Figure 3.35. *Editing the Operand property sheet*

Following this work, which can be done with a Scenario for the other OC, we can return to the Capability Blank diagram (OCB) to show all of the Actors/Entities, and then to add the relevant links.

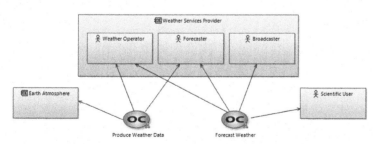

Figure 3.36. *Remainder and end of the Capability Blank diagram (OCB)*

Modeling work is fundamentally iterative and incremental!

Complete Example of Modeling with Capella: System Analysis

4.1. Main concepts and diagrams

Capella has a methodological guide in the form of the *Activity Explorer*. This lists the various activities and diagrams that can be carried out at the relevant engineering level, which in this case is System Analysis. Figure 4.1 shows the activities; throughout the case study we shall describe the different possible diagrams.

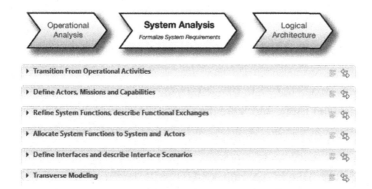

Figure 4.1. *Methodological activities of the "System Analysis" level*

NOTE.– Although Arcadia is a method, the modeling process remains completely flexible. The methodological activities presented in the

Activity Explorer are nearly all optional, and can be executed in any chosen order; the same is true for diagrams.

We shall therefore make another arbitrary – but reasoned – choice here in terms of the diagram realization. We start by defining high-level objectives, called System Capabilities. We shall expand on these Capabilities using Data Flow diagrams between Functions. Next we shall complete the System Analysis by producing the Architecture diagram, which involves allocating the Functions to the System or to the external Actors. We shall finish off the analysis with a description of the Scenarios, Modes and States, and by starting to model the data.

4.2. Going from the Operational level to the System level

The Operational Analysis shown previously involved creating a domain model, independently of the future system to be realized. The idea was to voluntarily create a level of abstraction from the system under study in order to focus on the "real" needs of the different stakeholders.

The System Analysis level, on the other hand, requires the following questions to be answered:

– What must the system do?

– What is the external interface of the system?

In order to answer the first question, the expected behavior is mainly modeled as Functions. We can obviously also make use of Scenarios and Mode and State diagrams, if necessary.

In order to answer the second question, all of the external Actors (human or not) and data/matter flows must be identified. The Architecture Blank diagram (SAB) will be very useful here for showing what enters the System from the Actors and what exits the System via the Actors.

Using all of the Operational Activities identified in Chapter 3 (those represented in the OAB of Figure 3.27, for example), a systematic approach is to ask whether each Activity will be realized by the system in its entirety, partially, or not at all. The result at the System Analysis level can be formalized as follows:

– entirely: the Activity becomes a Function of the same name, allocated to the System;

– partially: the Activity must be broken down into several Functions, some of which are allocated to the System and others to at least one Actor;

– not at all: the Activity becomes a Function of the same name, allocated to an Actor.

NOTE.– The decision to realize a given Activity is a project decision, influenced by the client requirements, budget, delays, technical feasibility, etc. Neither Arcadia nor Capella can make the decision on the architect's behalf.

If we apply this principle, starting with the OAB, a project meeting might lead to the decisions represented in Figure 4.2. Note that we have decided not to intervene in the forecast itself, which is always carried out by the forecaster. However, the system will have to provide a current situation, in the desired format, and recover the forecasts. This choice therefore entails interface requirements for the future system.

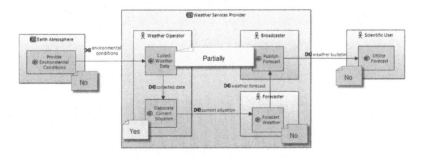

Figure 4.2. *Choice of Activity realization by the system. For a color version of the figure, see www.iste.co.uk/roques/arcadia.zip*

To initialize the System level while making the most of the work carried out at the Operational level, Capella provides a set of very useful tools, called "Transitions". These allow us to recover a System level Function from each of the Operational Activities while maintaining the flows, or an Actor of the System level from each of the Entities/Actors of the Operational level, etc.

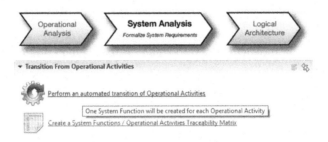

Figure 4.3. *Functional transition tool between Operational and System levels*

These transition commands can be accessed through the *Activity Explorer*, and more precisely in the contextual menu of a folder, or of a model element in the *Project Explorer*. The user can control what the tool creates at the System level with great precision by selecting a subset of possible elements in a Diff/merge type dialog window. In simple cases, this can be done by clicking the *Apply* button to select and apply everything without making any changes.

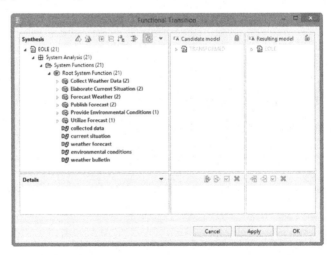

Figure 4.4. *Dialog window for functional transition between Operational and System levels*

NOTE.– All of the transitions proposed by Capella are top/down, going toward the engineering level that is immediately inferior. It must be noted that the transitions are iterative and incremental, which is very handy for complex projects. If a System Function, or even an Operational Activity, is found to be missing during work on the Physical Architecture, good practice would involve adding the missing element to the highest relevant level, and then applying several successive transitions in order to recover the lowest level where it is missing. The tool does not erase the additions and refinements brought to the lower levels.

By clicking on *Apply*, a new window appears, listing all of the transformations to be carried out on the model. In our case, Capella creates System level Functions and Functional Exchanges, but also Function Ports to link the Functional Exchanges. While Operational Activities do not have ports in order to maximize simplicity, from the System level onward, Functions possess function input or output Ports, to which the Functional Exchanges are connected.

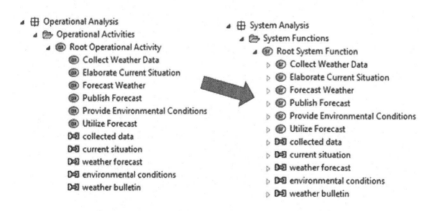

Figure 4.5. *Result of functional transition in the Project Explorer*

In order to check whether Capella has properly created the Ports and added a realization link to each Activity, we select one of the System level Functions in the *Semantic Browser*. Here, we can clearly see the new input and output Ports, as well as the realization link to the Operational Activity of the same name.

Figure 4.6. *Result of functional transition in the Semantic Browser*

4.3. System Capabilities

The Operational Analysis above involved creating a domain model, independently of the future system to be realized. The idea was to voluntarily create a level of abstraction from the system under study in order to focus on the "real" needs of the different stakeholders. Following a project meeting like the one mentioned in section 4.2, we decide to leave the forecasting activity outside of the system, at least for the first version.

NOTE.– Operational Analysis is useful for referring to the "need" in its entirety, independently of the realization choices made at any given moment. This allows opportunities to be identified for subsequent system versions, i.e. preparing the work of weather forecasting, or even controlling it fully, as soon as this becomes possible technologically (computational power, artificial intelligence, etc.).

In our example, System Capabilities are less extensive than Operational Capabilities in terms of cover. However, here we can also use a transition command in order to benefit from automatic realization links.

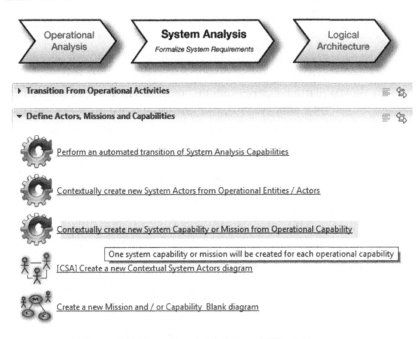

Figure 4.7. *Transition tool of Capabilities between Operational and System levels*

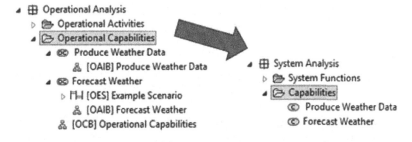

Figure 4.8. *Result of transition of Capabilities in the Project Explorer*

Now we only have to rename the second Capability to reduce its field of action. We can call it: "Broadcast Weather Forecast". Just like for the Operational level, we will start by working on the Data Flow diagrams, here between Functions, called SDFB. This is particularly important as there are Functions that must be broken down due to partial allocation to the system.

NOTE (Arcadia Rule).– Only "leaf" Functions (those that are not broken down) can have input/output Ports. As soon as a Function is broken down into subfunctions, we therefore have to work on the assignment of Functional Exchanges to the subfunctions of the parent Function.

Let us create two contextual diagrams, one for each System Capability, through the contextual menu in the Project Explorer (*New Diagram/Table... System Data Flow Blank*). Note that this way, the diagram automatically takes on the name of each Capability. This can be checked in the *Diagrams Viewer*, on the right of the *Activity Explorer* window.

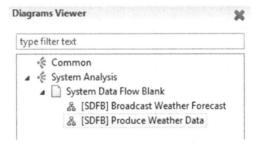

Figure 4.9. *Result of the creation of diagrams in the Diagram Viewer*

4.4. Functional Analysis at the System level

For the first Capability, "Produce Weather Data", the central Function is "Collect Weather Data". Instead of manually inserting the Functions that can be chosen using the palette's *Insert/Remove Functions* button, we can instead ask Capella to automatically create the SDFB by inserting the Function, as well as all those connected to it. To do this, the diagram must be made contextual to the chosen Function using a property field of the diagram: *Contextual Elements*.

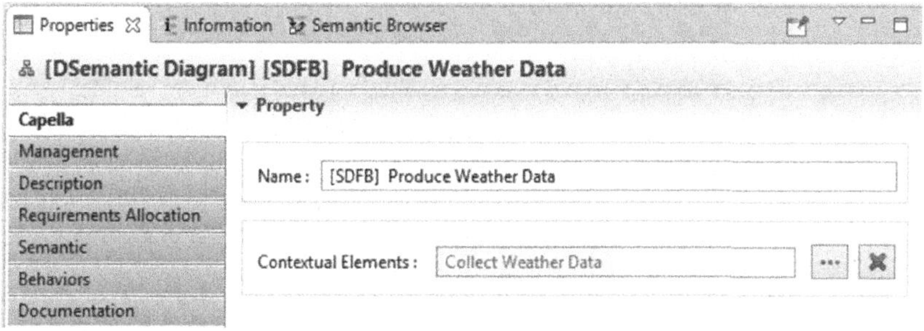

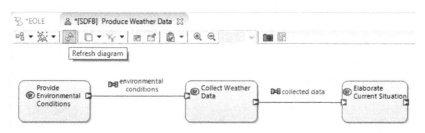

Figure 4.10. *Diagram made contextual to a chosen Function*

Asking Capella to refresh the diagram (F5 key or *Refresh diagram* button from the top bar) will automatically fill the diagram. After a couple of quick touches to improve the graphical representation, we obtain Figure 4.11.

Figure 4.11. *Result of refreshing the contextual diagram. For a color version of the figure, see www.iste.co.uk/roques/arcadia.zip*

NOTE.– As opposed to a classical *Blank*, the contextual diagram is updated automatically. In particular, as soon as a new Function has additional Exchanges with "Collect Weather Data", it automatically appears in this contextual SDFB, which it would not have otherwise.

We must now keep up our work by breaking down the "Collect" Function and by working on the Functional Exchanges, since only leaf Functions can have Ports. This is the only case where we recommend changing the fill color of a Function: for broken down Functions, we recommend changing them to white in order to differentiate them properly.

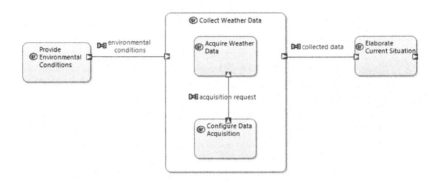

Figure 4.12. *Start of functional breakdown. For a color version of the figure, see www.iste.co.uk/roques/arcadia.zip*

Just after the first breakdown step, we must check that the model validation highlights the expected errors. As anticipated, there are transition warnings, marking that the elements of the System level have not been realized by the elements of the Logical Architecture level. There are also warnings telling us that the Functions have not yet been allocated. There are two new warnings regarding the Ports of the parent Function that must be delegated to its subfunctions.

Message	Level	Rule id	R
▲ 🗁 Capella (35 items)			
▲ 🗁 Design (9 items)			
▲ 🗁 Completeness (9 items)			
ⓢ The leaf "Acquire Weather Data"(SystemFunction) is not allocated by any Component.	⚠ Warning	DCOM_03	
ⓢ The leaf "Configure Data Acquisition"(SystemFunction) is not allocated by any Component.	⚠ Warning	DCOM_03	
ⓢ The leaf "Elaborate Current Situation"(SystemFunction) is not allocated by any Component.	⚠ Warning	DCOM_03	
ⓢ The leaf "Forecast Weather"(SystemFunction) is not allocated by any Component.	⚠ Warning	DCOM_03	
ⓢ The leaf "Provide Environmental Conditions"(SystemFunction) is not allocated by any Component.	⚠ Warning	DCOM_03	
ⓢ The leaf "Publish Forecast"(SystemFunction) is not allocated by any Component.	⚠ Warning	DCOM_03	
ⓢ The leaf "Utilize Forecast"(SystemFunction) is not allocated by any Component.	⚠ Warning	DCOM_03	
▷◁ The source of "collected data" (Functional Exchange) is not delegated to a leaf System Function	⚠ Warning	DCOM_20	
▷◁ The target of "environmental conditions" (Functional Exchange) is not delegated to a leaf System Function	⚠ Warning	DCOM_20	
▷ 🗁 Transition (26 items)			

Figure 4.13. *Results of validation after the start of functional breakdown*

The model becomes correct simply by moving the Ports of the parent Function toward subfunction "Acquire".

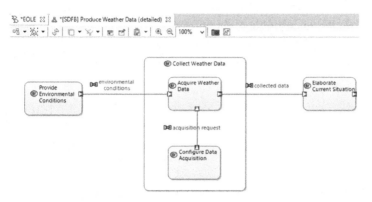

Figure 4.14. *End of functional breakdown on SDFB. For a color version of the figure, see www.iste.co.uk/roques/arcadia.zip*

An advantage of Capella is that it allows the modeler to keep showing the parent Function without its subfunctions on a higher level diagram, aimed at a different audience. This can be achieved by cloning the diagram (from the *Diagrams Viewer*) and using the *Insert/Remove Functions* button of the palette inside the parent Function. Capella then shows the Ports of the subfunctions on the boundary of the parent Function. The model is unchanged, as it is only a calculated graphical representation. This can be verified by the activating the *Semantic Browser*.

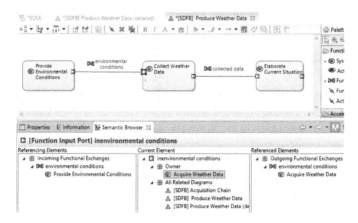

Figure 4.15. *SDFB showing higher level view (without subfunctions). For a color version of the figure, see www.iste.co.uk/roques/arcadia.zip*

In a similar fashion, let us make a second contextual SDFB around the second Function to be broken down: "Publish forecast".

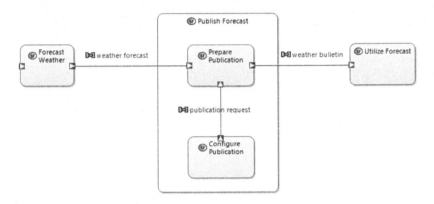

Figure 4.16. *Second functional breakdown diagram. For a color version of the figure, see www.iste.co.uk/roques/arcadia.zip*

NOTE.– Note that these two SDFB diagrams involve different Functions. In the free version of Capella, only one person can modify the model at any given moment: the tool is said to be a "single user" tool. A multiuser version also exists: Team for Capella [BON 16], which is distributed by Obeo (www.obeo.fr/en/capella-professional-offer). This version would have allowed us to create both diagrams in parallel in the same model.

Note also that the appearance of a Function in the functional diagram attached to a Capability implies the automatic creation of a semantic exploitation link between this Function and the Capability. The *Involved Functions* field in the properties field of a Capability is thus filled automatically by Capella, and the link can be seen in the *Semantic Browser*.

We will now create a third SDFB that gathers together all of the leaf Functions in order to visualize the System level global data flow.

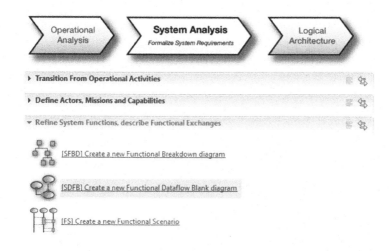

Figure 4.17. *Creation of a new Data Flow diagram (SDFB)*

This can be achieved with only a few clicks with Capella. Once the empty diagram has been created using the *Activity Explorer*, we insert all of the leaf Functions into the diagram using the *Selection Wizard* of the transfer dialog.

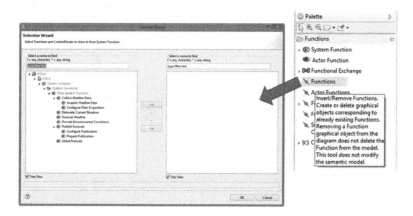

Figure 4.18. *Insertion of all leaf Functions in the global SDFB*

We use the double arrow to move all of the Functions to the right, and then move the two broken-down Functions back to the left.

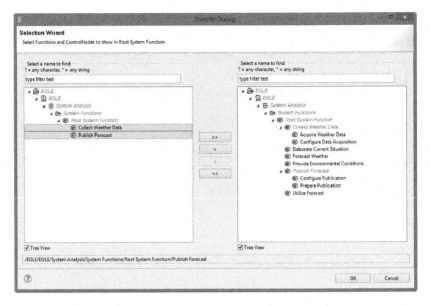

Figure 4.19. *Removing the non-leaf Functions in global SDFB*

Activating the *Arrange Selection* command in all of the graphical objects present in the diagram, or using the *Arrange All* command, immediately results in a usable diagram.

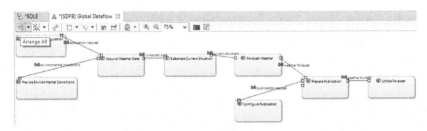

Figure 4.20. *Initial version of global SDFB. For a color version of the figure, see www.iste.co.uk/roques/arcadia.zip*

Resizing the Functions and slightly moving the ports quickly provides us with a graphical oversight that we can work with. In the meantime, we can check that there are not unused Ports, as the diagram is no longer partial, unlike the two previous ones.

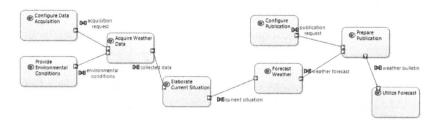

Figure 4.21. *Improved version of global SDFB. For a color version of the figure, see www.iste.co.uk/roques/arcadia.zip*

4.5. Functional Chains at the System level

Functional data flow refers to all of the dependencies that exist between Functions. A Functional Chain represents a set path in this global data flow. It is particularly useful for describing the expected behavior of the system in a given context, and therefore for piloting verification/validation tests. Functional Chains are also often used to express non-functional constraints in functional paths, such as latency, criticality, confidentiality, redundancy, etc.

To create a Functional Chain with Capella, a succession of Functional Exchanges must be selected (the source and target Functions are selected implicitly), and then the contextual menu must be activated.

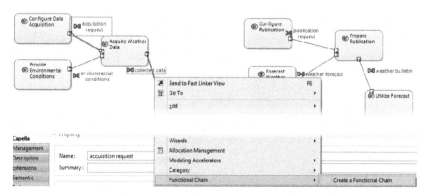

Figure 4.22. *Creation of a Functional Chain in an SDFB. For a color version of the figure, see www.iste.co.uk/roques/arcadia.zip*

This results in both a new modeling element, represented by a square and called FunctionalChain 1, and graphical additions to the data flow. The source Function is surrounded, as is the target Function, and arrows are added between the input and output Ports of the intermediate Functions in order to materialize the direction of the selected path.

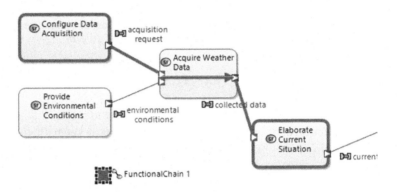

Figure 4.23. *Results of the creation of a Functional Chain. For a color version of the figure, see www.iste.co.uk/roques/arcadia.zip*

Note that the Functional Chain can be found in the *Project Explorer* under the technical element *Root System Function*, at the same level as the System Functions.

To modify an existing Functional Chain, a specific contextual diagram, called a Functional Chain Description, must be used. This diagram can be created with a right click of *New Diagram/Table* on the square, or on the element in the *Project Explorer*.

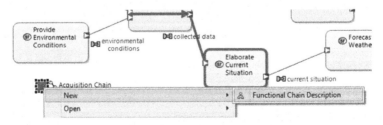

Figure 4.24. *Contextual creation of a Functional Chain Description diagram. For a color version of the figure, see www.iste.co.uk/roques/arcadia.zip*

The diagram obtained is quite unique. It is always synchronized with the current state of the Chain's definition in the model. The model elements present in the diagram are not themselves Functions and Functional Exchanges, but rather references to these elements, called *Functional Chain Involvement*.

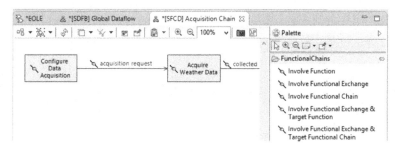

Figure 4.25. *Description diagram of a Functional Chain. For a color version of the figure, see www.iste.co.uk/roques/arcadia.zip*

We can therefore add or remove "links" in order to modify the Chain. Let us take a look at what happens if we destroy the central link of the acquisition Chain. To do this, the command *Delete From Model* must be applied to the Functional Chain Involvement called "Acquire".

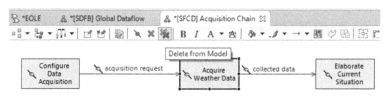

Figure 4.26. *Destruction of a link in an FCD. For a color version of the figure, see www.iste.co.uk/roques/arcadia.zip*

NOTE.– The command *Delete From Diagram* is not active in this type of diagram, just like in the Blank. As the diagram is still synchronized, the elements would automatically reappear when it is opened again. The confirmation window following *Delete From Model* shows that it is indeed the links that are being destroyed, and not the Functions or Exchanges.

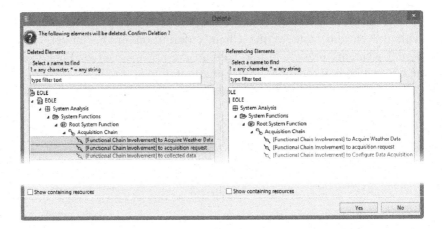

Figure 4.27. *Delete from model in an FCD*

By opening the global SDFB, we can see that the Functional Chain has automatically been updated. Moreover, the tool clearly shows that the chain is now invalid.

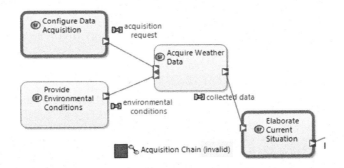

Figure 4.28. *Invalid Functional Chain shown in an SDFB. For a color version of the figure, see www.iste.co.uk/roques/arcadia.zip*

Using the command *Undo*, we can return to the previous, valid, state of the Functional Chain. In fact, we want to add the Function "Provide Env. Conditions" and the associated Exchange at the entrance to the Chain. To do this, the Function must first be added to the Chain using the command *Involve Function*, and then the Exchange is added using the command *Involve Functional Exchange*.

Note that the tool only proposes Exchanges that already exist in the model.

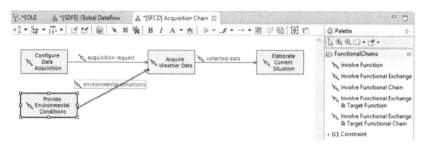

Figure 4.29. *Adding links to an FCD. For a color version of the figure, see www.iste.co.uk/roques/arcadia.zip*

NOTE.– A link in a Functional Chain can be another Functional Chain. Use the *Involve Functional Chain* command to insert an existing Chain into a new overarching Chain. This approach is very useful in bottom-up assembly of reusable Physical Components that have their own simple Chains and contribute to the creation of a composite Functional Chain.

Going back to the Data Flow diagram, we can see that the Functional Chain has automatically been updated.

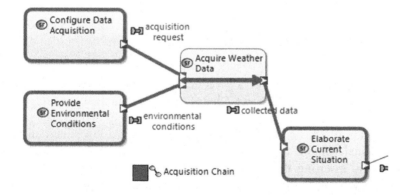

Figure 4.30. *Modified Functional Chain updated in the SDFB. For a color version of the figure, see www.iste.co.uk/roques/arcadia.zip*

NOTE.– We have seen that a Functional Chain can become invalid following the modification of its constituent model elements. It can also appear as incomplete in a diagram, for example if the command *Delete From Diagram* is applied to one of its links. Remember that the command *Delete From Diagram* does not modify the model, but acts only on the graphical objects present in the current diagram.

Removing one of the chain's functions from the previous SDFB causes the tool to consider it incomplete, after a *Refresh Diagram*.

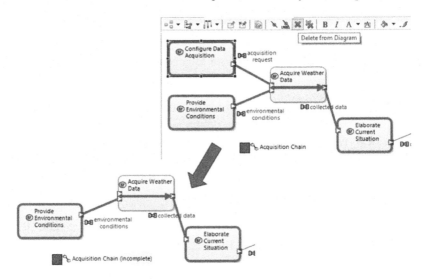

Figure 4.31. *Incomplete Functional Chain shown in an SDFB. For a color version of the figure, see www.iste.co.uk/roques/arcadia.zip*

We will also create a second Functional Chain, involving publication this time. The two Chains can appear in the same diagram.

It can often be useful to create one Data Flow diagram per Functional Chain for the purpose of documentation. Instead of manually inserting the Functions and Exchanges that participate in a given Chain, Capella allows us to automatically create this type of diagram by using a command from the palette of the group Accelerators called *Functional Chain Elements*. After choosing the Chain involved in the selection dialog, the command *Arrange*

Selection is applied, and Capella produces the minimal diagram containing only the elements that belong to the Chain.

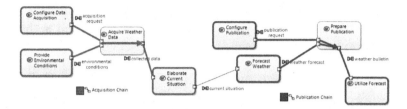

Figure 4.32. *SDFB showing two Functional Chains. For a color version of the figure, see www.iste.co.uk/roques/arcadia.zip*

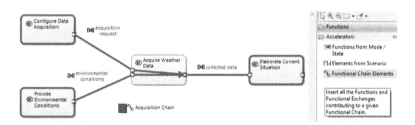

Figure 4.33. *SDFB of a Functional Chain created automatically by an Accelerator. For a color version of the figure, see www.iste.co.uk/roques/arcadia.zip*

NOTE.– If we want the diagram to be updated when the Functional Chain is modified, we must remember to make it contextual by once again using *Contextual Elements*. Otherwise, seeing as the diagram involved is a Blank, any new Functions involved in the chain will not be shown automatically.

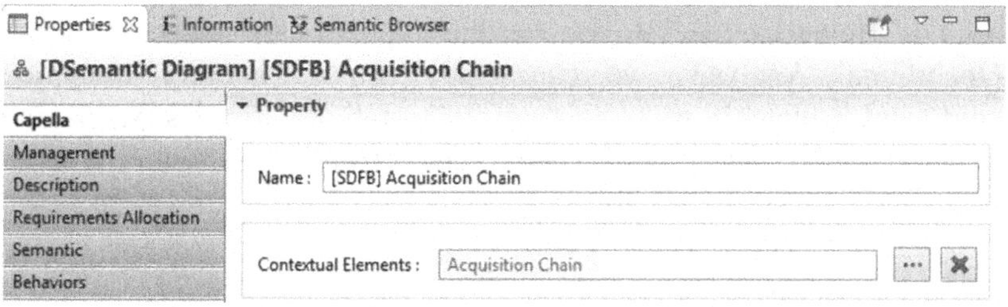

Figure 4.34. *SDFB of a Functional Chain made contextual*

4.6. Allocation of Functions to the System or to Actors

In order to continue the Functional Analysis, we must now carry out Function Allocation. At the System Analysis level, Functions can only be allocated to the System itself, which is considered a "black box", or to one of the external Actors.

For the moment, there are no Actors at this level: the Actors folder is empty; however, Capella automatically creates a model element called System when the project is first initialized. We can rename it EOLE for example.

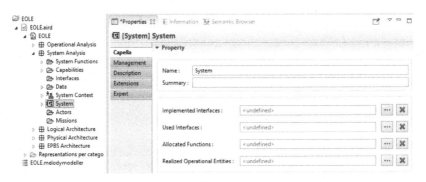

Figure 4.35. *System model element in the Project Explorer*

Several possibilities are available for creating the Actors (as is often the case). Obviously the Actors of the System level could be manually created directly in the Architecture Blank diagram (SAB), or beforehand in another more specific diagram, called Contextual System Actors (CSA), or even in a Capabilities Diagram (CB, or MCB). However, seeing as we have previously carried out an Operational Analysis, we can make use of another transition command, which allows us to recover Operational Entities/Actors and to automatically make them Actors at the System level, with the same name and realization link for each.

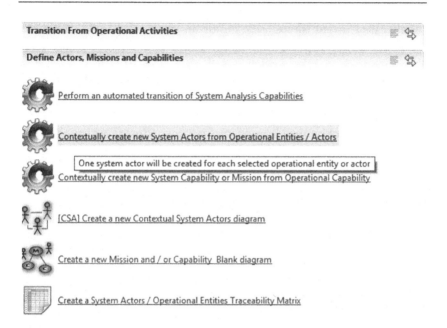

Figure 4.36. *Actor transition tool between Operational and System levels*

The user can control what the tool creates at the System level, first by selecting a subset of Operational Entities/Actors in a selection dialog, and later more precisely by selecting elements in a *Diff/merge* dialog window. Here, the first window allows us to reject the entity "Weather Services Provider", which does not interact directly with the System (but only through the human profiles that it contains). To do this, we must allow for multiple disjointed selections through the *Ctrl* key.

In simple cases, the user can directly click on the *Apply* button to select everything. Here, we shall use this to illustrate finer ways of guiding the transition. By default, Capella offers to keep the same allocations between Functions and System Actors as those present at the Operational level. As a result, keeping the same allocations for the Activities that we have decided to have carried out by the system only partially (such as "Collect Weather Data"), or completely (such as

"Elaborate Current Situation"), is not desirable. We could of course apply all of the proposed transformations, and modify the allocations that propagate to the System level. We will use the *Diff/merge* interface in order to only propagate those allocations of Activities carried out completely by the Actors, i.e. "Forecast Weather", "Provide Environmental Conditions" and "Utilize Forecast". To do this, we shall act on the *Component Function Allocation* elements that appear under the Actors in the left window.

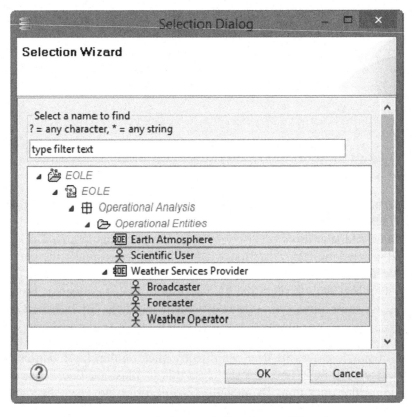

Figure 4.37. *Selection window for transition of Actors between Operational and System levels*

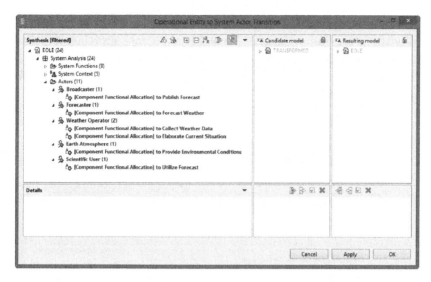

Figure 4.38. *Dialog window for transition of Actors between Operational and System levels*

The allocations for undesired Functions must be removed by selecting them, and then in the central window (*Candidate model*) ticking the *Ignore on the left* button. They then disappear from the left area.

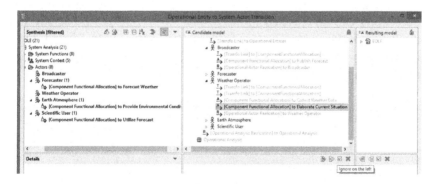

Figure 4.39. *Removing some of the allocation transitions*

If we now apply the changes by clicking on *OK*, the undesired allocations are not propagated. To be certain before applying, it is also possible to see the result beforehand. This can be done by clicking on the command *Copy all to the right*, which fills the window on the right (*Resulting Model*).

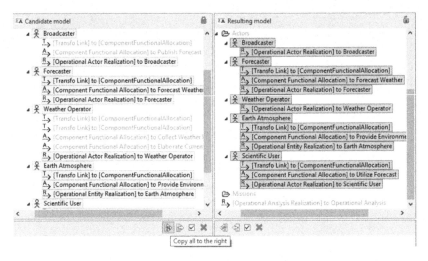

Figure 4.40. *Prediction of the transition result*

In order to verify the correct application of the transitions, everything can be checked in the *Project Explorer*, and especially in the *Semantic Browser*. The five System Actors have been created, and if these are selected one by one, we can see if a Function has been allocated to them or not.

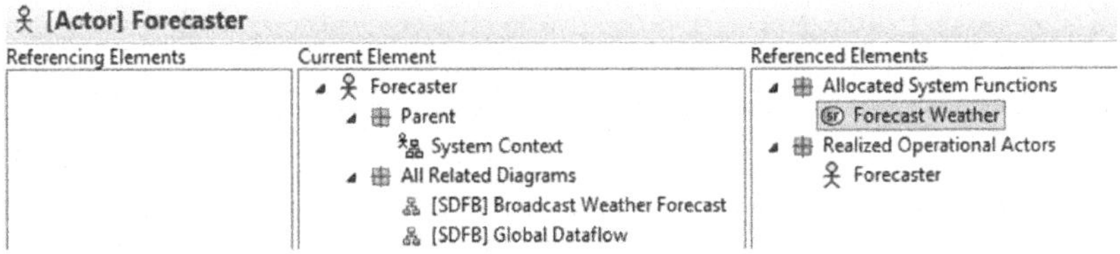

Figure 4.41. *Verification of the result of transition*

We can now proceed to allocating the remaining Functions. The most obvious way of doing this is to create an Architecture Blank diagram (SAB) and to graphically allocate the Functions in the System or the Actors using the *Manage Function Allocation* command from the SAB palette.

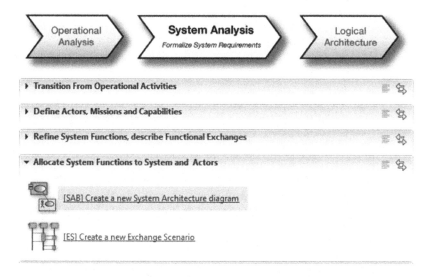

Figure 4.42. *Creation of an Architecture Blank diagram at the System level (SAB)*

NOTE.– Although the SAB is a *Blank* diagram, it is not empty. Capella works perfectly in tune with Arcadia and knows that it would be pointless to realize an Architecture diagram at this level without showing the System. As a result, Capella inserts it automatically so that we do not need to. However, the SAB can be partial: we must choose which Actors we want to show.

We decide to insert all of the Actors: we will make a global diagram, given the low level of complexity of the subject. We can always simplify the SAB later, by cloning it and splitting it into groups of Actors, or by applying filters.

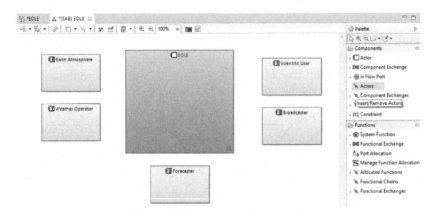

Figure 4.43. *Start of Architecture Blank diagram (SAB). For a color version of the figure, see www.iste.co.uk/roques/arcadia.zip*

We can already start by inserting the Functions allocated to the Actors by transition. Capella provides a shortcut for this: the *Insert All Allocated Functions* command in the palette under the command *Insert Allocated Functions*.

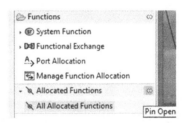

Figure 4.44. *Example of command list in the palette*

NOTE.– Remember that an arrowhead in front of a command from the palette means that similar commands are available by "opening" the arrow. The list can then be "pinned", using the *Pin Open* button located on the right.

With a single click at the back of the diagram from the command *Insert All Allocated Functions* (outside of the Actors and of the System), Capella inserts all of the allocated Functions to all of the elements. If we had clicked inside an Actor, Capella would have inserted all of the Functions allocated to this Actor, without proposing a dialog window that would have appeared with the other command, *Insert Allocated Functions*.

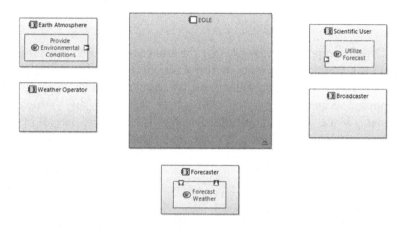

Figure 4.45. *More of the Architecture Blank diagram (SAB). For a color version of the figure, see www.iste.co.uk/roques/arcadia.zip*

We can now move on to allocating the remaining Functions. This is achieved by graphically allocating the Functions in the System or the Actors with the button *Manage Function Allocation* from the SAB palette. Note that Functional Exchanges automatically appear as soon as the target and source Functions are present in the diagram.

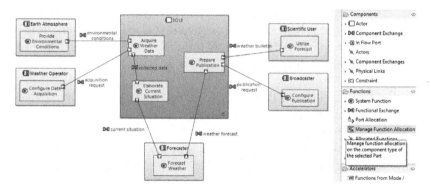

Figure 4.46. *Function allocation in the Architecture Blank diagram (SAB). For a color version of the figure, see www.iste.co.uk/roques/arcadia.zip*

NOTE (Arcadia Rule).– Only "leaf" Functions (Functions that are not broken down) can be allocated. As soon as a Function is broken down into subfunctions, it can no longer be selected in the allocation dialog windows. Arcadia does not allow a Function to be allocated several times either.

Capella imposes these rules in the allocation dialogs, helping to avoid methodological errors in construction. To check that we have allocated all of the system Functions, we can therefore try to apply the command *Manage Function Allocation* again to any structural element. If the choice of selection is empty, this means that all of the Functions have been allocated. The model validation can, of course, also be used.

We still need to allocate the Functional Exchanges. In the same way that the Functions must be allocated to the System and to the Actors, we must also allocate the Functional Exchanges to structural links between the System and the Actors, called Component Exchanges.

NOTE (Arcadia Rule).– At every level of Arcadia, a Functional Exchange between two Functions allocated to two Behavioral Components must be allocated to a single Component Exchange between these two Components. This Component Exchange references all of the Functional Exchanges that it implements. In general, a Component Exchange is made up of a synthesis of several Functional Exchanges that it implements and gathers together. The direction of the Component Exchange is purely conventional, but the general rule is that the direction of the Exchange is from the provider toward the user of the main data exchanged.

Before carrying out this work, we shall make our model slightly more complex by adding a "Subscribe" Function for the user and a "Manage Subscriptions" Function in EOLE. This can be done directly in the SAB, without having to go back into a Data Flow diagram (or any other type of diagram).

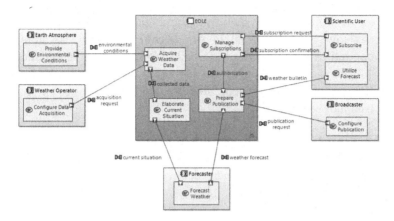

Figure 4.47. *Adding subscription management to the SAB. For a color version of the figure, see www.iste.co.uk/roques/arcadia.zip*

We have created two Functions and three Functional Exchanges to start representing the management of subscriptions in a simple manner. We must also add the Function "Manage Subscriptions" into the Functional Chain of publication. This can be done by editing the corresponding SFCD.

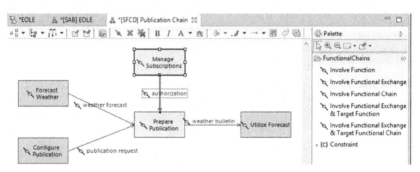

Figure 4.48. *Updating the publication Chain. For a color version of the figure, see www.iste.co.uk/roques/arcadia.zip*

NOTE.– In Figure 4.48, some of the Functions are no longer green, unlike what has been the case in all of the diagrams so far. The reason for this is that, since some of the Functions have been allocated to Actors, Capella represents them automatically in the same color as the Actors, so light blue. It is important to distinguish the Functions under the responsibility of the System from those that are allocated to external Actors. However, apart from in Architecture diagrams, no graphical clue can tell us this: as a result, Capella takes care of it automatically. This is yet another reason to not manually change the color of the Functions in diagrams, except possibly for broken-down Functions, which cannot be allocated.

While we are here, if we open up the global SDFB again, we can see that the publication Chain is now marked as incomplete, since the Blank diagram is not automatically updated when Functions are added.

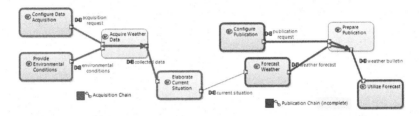

Figure 4.49. *Global SDFB with incomplete publication chain. For a color version of the figure, see www.iste.co.uk/roques/arcadia.zip*

We need to insert the new Functions in order to preserve the exhaustive aspect of this particular diagram. Note that if we had made a specific diagram for the publication Chain, and if we had made it contextual to the chain, it would automatically be updated and complete.

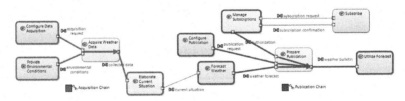

Figure 4.50. *Completed global SDFB. For a color version of the figure, see www.iste.co.uk/roques/arcadia.zip*

Let us go back to the allocation of Functional Exchanges to Component Exchanges. We must start creating a first Component Exchange between the weather operator and EOLE. We use the

Component Exchange tool of the palette, which by default creates a Component Exchange and two Ports in the direction of the line.

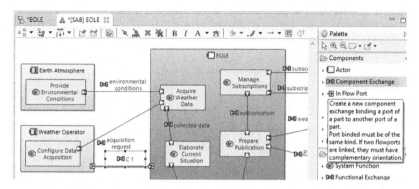

Figure 4.51. *Creation of a first Component Exchange in the SAB. For a color version of the figure, see www.iste.co.uk/roques/arcadia.zip*

We rename this Component Exchange, for example "Weather Operator HMI", and follow on by allocating it the Functional Exchange "acquisition request". If we later add an EOLE response to the model, or image requests, etc., we can pass all of these functional flows through the same Component Exchange, as long as they have similar non-functional properties.

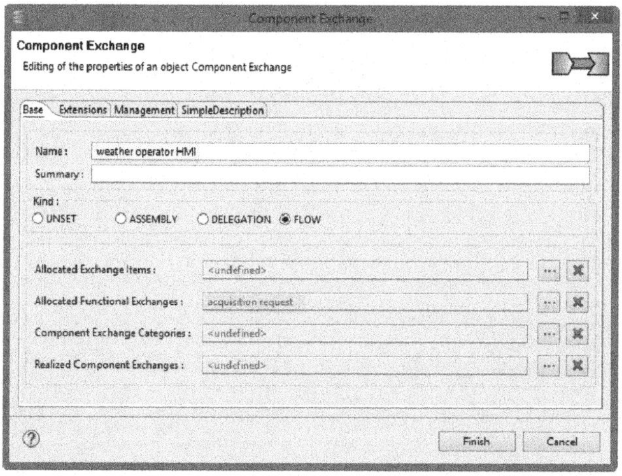

Figure 4.52. *Property sheet of a Component Exchange*

The allocation relation appears in the diagram as dotted lines linking the Function Ports to the Component Ports.

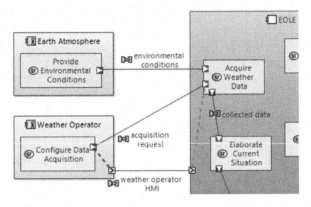

Figure 4.53. *Exchange allocation in the SAB. For a color version of the figure, see www.iste.co.uk/roques/arcadia.zip*

Another way of creating Component Exchanges is to ask Capella via a Modeling Accelerator called *Component Exchanges*. This automatically creates a Component Exchange by Functional Exchange, giving it the same name and realizing the allocation.

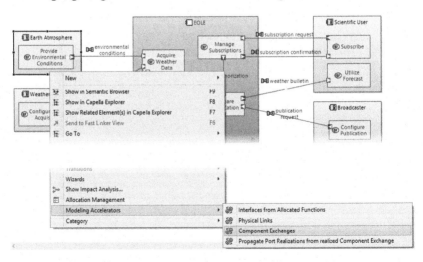

Figure 4.54. *Creation of a Component Exchange through an Accelerator. For a color version of the figure, see www.iste.co.uk/roques/arcadia.zip*

The result is immediate. We might need to rename the Component Exchange, especially if it gathers several of the Functional Exchanges.

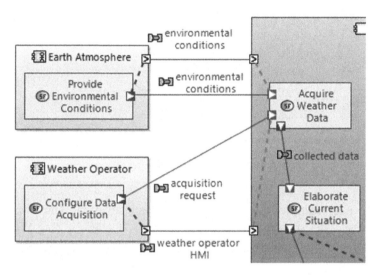

Figure 4.55. *Result of the creation of a Component Exchange by Accelerator. For a color version of the figure, see www.iste.co.uk/roques/arcadia.zip*

There are two functional flows that circulate between the forecaster and EOLE. We can therefore choose to make them both pass through the same bidirectional Component Exchange, or on the contrary to make each of them to pass through a different Component Exchange. The question is the following: do these functional flows have different non-functional properties (volume, frequency, confidentiality, etc.)? If they do, it is better to separate the Component Exchanges, otherwise there is no need.

NOTE (Arcadia Rule).– Arcadia demands that Functional Exchanges be unidirectional. A Function Port is either an input or an output, and this property cannot be modified in Capella. On the other hand, a Component Exchange can be uni- or bi-directional. In fact, it is the Component Ports whose direction property can be edited: *in, out, inout.*

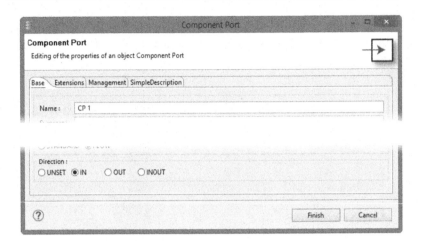

Figure 4.56. *Property sheet of a Component Port*

In our example, the two flows: "current situation" and "weather forecast" are similar in terms of volume, frequency, etc. We can therefore decide to go through the same bidirectional Component Exchange.

To create this exchange, there are two options, which are equal in terms of the number of clicks and speed:

– create a unidirectional Exchange with the palette, and then modify each of the Ports by going through an inout;

– first create two bidirectional Ports with the palette, and then an Exchange going through these two Ports.

We can then rename the Component Exchange and allocate it both functional flows. In the same way, we can also create a unidirectional Component Exchange between "Broadcaster" and EOLE.

We have significantly advanced the allocation of Functional Exchanges to Component Exchanges. Our example here was made quite simple on purpose. Imagine a real project with several dozen Functional Exchanges: how can we easily find out if we have forgotten to allocate some of the Functional Exchanges? In Capella diagrams there exists a number of filters, depending on the level of engineering and the type of diagram. Most of these filters aim to simplify the diagrams for publication, and later we shall look at how these are used, but some of them are aimed more at highlighting the level of progress of the diagram, and as a result are only temporary. To answer the previous question, we can ask Capella to temporarily hide the Functional Exchanges that have already been allocated in order to show only those that still need to be allocated. As soon as the work is done, we can take the filter off. This filter is located in the top panel, which appears when the diagram has been selected. It is called *Hide Allocated Functional Exchanges*.

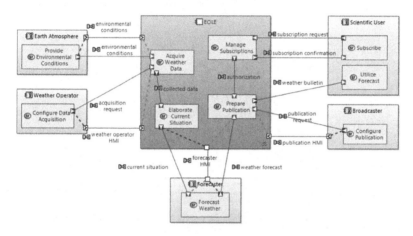

Figure 4.57. *SAB in intermediate state. For a color version of the figure, see www.iste.co.uk/roques/arcadia.zip*

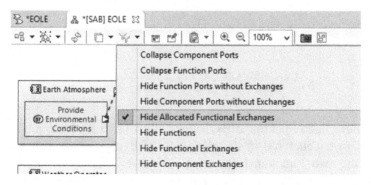

Figure 4.58. *Apply a temporary filter to the SAB*

After the filter has been applied, only the three Functional Exchanges between the scientific user and EOLE are shown.

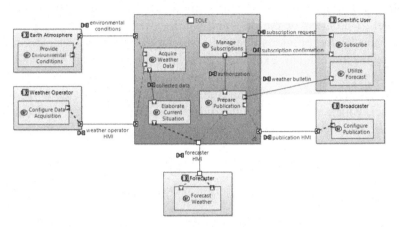

Figure 4.59. *Filter applied to intermediate SAB. For a color version of the figure, see www.iste.co.uk/roques/arcadia.zip*

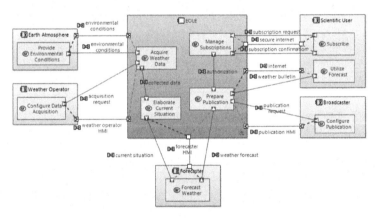

Figure 4.60. *Complete SAB. For a color version of the figure, see www.iste.co.uk/roques/arcadia.zip*

These three Functional Exchanges allow us to illustrate a classical problem encountered in the allocation of Exchanges. Let us assume that the two Functional Exchanges involved in subscriptions must absolutely be secure, as money might be involved, while this might not be the case for the last Functional Exchange. There is therefore a good reason to separate these Functional Exchanges into two different Component Exchanges, one secure and the other not. This way, we can visually represent different interface requirements. Once the filter is removed, we are left with the complete SAB.

NOTE.– A Function can only be allocated once. Similarly, a Functional Exchange can only be allocated to one Component Exchange. Once the weather bulletin has been allocated to the Internet, as in the previous example, Capella only offers the two other Functional Exchanges for the secure Internet.

In our simple example the complete diagram is still printable, but for a complex project this is rarely the case. A way must therefore be found to publish partial versions of the complete diagram, providing coherent content for a specific predefined reader type. A first solution would be to make a split along the two Functional Chains.

To achieve this, we can clone the diagram twice, insert each Functional Chain into a cloned diagram, and then delete from the diagram all of the elements that do not participate in the chain involved. To make each diagram clearer, we can then apply the filters: *Hide Function Ports without Exchanges, Hide Component Ports without Exchanges*. This quickly results in the following two partial diagrams (Figure 4.61 and 4.62).

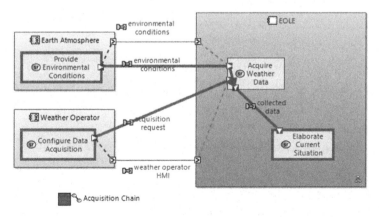

Figure 4.61. *Partial SAB on the acquisition Chain. For a color version of the figure, see www.iste.co.uk/roques/arcadia.zip*

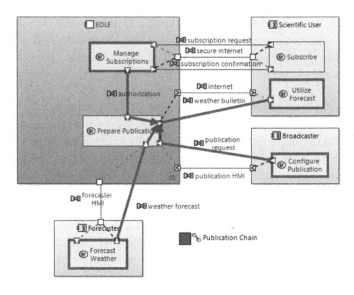

Figure 4.62. *Partial SAB on the publication Chain. For a color version of the figure, see www.iste.co.uk/roques/arcadia.zip*

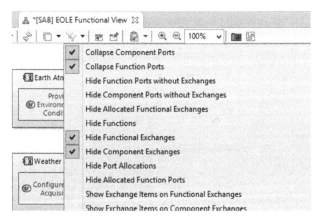

Figure 4.63. *Filters for a purely functional view of the SAB*

Another possibility involves keeping all of the Actors, but deleting different types of model elements from the diagram. For example, we can provide a purely functional view of the System by hiding all of the Exchanges and all of the Ports. Only a few seconds are needed to apply the four filters shown in Figure 4.63 to a new clone of the SAB, and thus to obtain a purely functional view of the System.

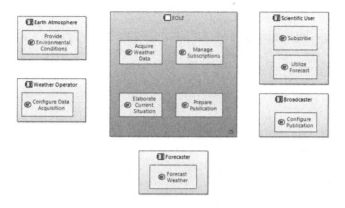

Figure 4.64. *Purely functional view of the SAB. For a color version of the figure, see www.iste.co.uk/roques/arcadia.zip*

On the other hand, in a new SAB we can choose to hide the Functions so as to only show the Component Exchanges. With a single click (by selecting the filter *Hide Functions*), we immediately obtain Figure 4.65, which shows the external interface of the System.

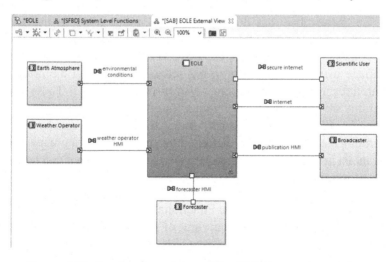

Figure 4.65. *Purely external view of the SAB. For a color version of the figure, see www.iste.co.uk/roques/arcadia.zip*

An interesting possibility involves asking Capella to show the names of the allocated Functional Exchanges instead of those of the Component Exchanges. This is done by applying an extra filter, *Show Allocated Functional Exchanges on Component Exchanges*, and then refreshing the diagram.

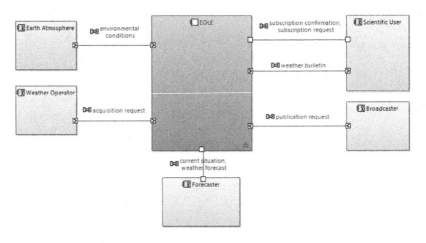

Figure 4.66. *Extended external view of the SAB. For a color version of the figure, see www.iste.co.uk/roques/arcadia.zip*

NOTE.– Remember that it is often useful to be able to distinguish between the work diagrams and the diagrams used for communicating. A work diagram can be complex, but can be used by the modeler as a complete overview, shown on a big screen, while using the graphical capabilities of the tool: zoom, *Outline* window, etc. These work diagrams are not meant to be communicated, and even less printed. The modeler will have to extract from them the diagrams to be communicated by using the cloning, masking and filtering capabilities of Capella in order to provide each reader with the relevant and required level of information.

To finish off this part of the Functional Analysis, we ask the tool to automatically generate the tree view of the functional breakdown at the System level. To do this, we go back to the *Activity Explorer* and ask for a *Functional Breakdown diagram* (SFBD).

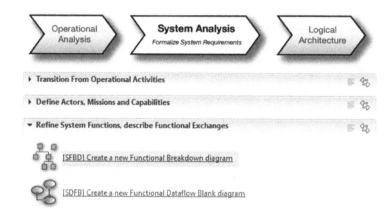

Figure 4.67. *Creating a Functional Breakdown Diagram at the System level (SFBD)*

NOTE.– The Breakdown diagram behaves oppositely to Blank diagrams. It is not created empty, and instead automatically contains all of the relevant model elements of the type involved (at the Arcadia level involved). Moreover, it is systemically updated when a new model element is created in another diagram or from the Project Explorer.

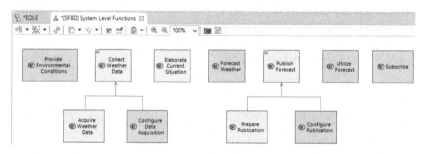

Figure 4.68. *System level Functional Breakdown Diagram (SFBD). For a color version of the figure, see www.iste.co.uk/roques/arcadia.zip*

Remember that the Functions in light blue are those that have been allocated to the Actors. Good practice involves manually changing the color of the parent Functions that can no longer be allocated to white, such as "Collect" and "Publish" in our example. In this way, the only Functions that are still in green are those allocated to the System.

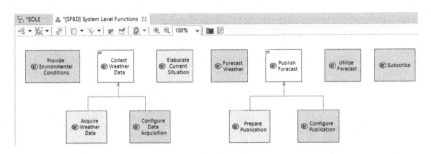

Figure 4.69. *Modified Functional Breakdown Diagram (SFBD). For a color version of the figure, see www.iste.co.uk/roques/arcadia.zip*

4.7. System-level Scenarios

We have already seen that Capella provides several types of Scenario diagrams at each level of Arcadia:

– Functional Scenarios (FSs): the lifelines are Functions;

– Exchange Scenarios (ESs): the lifelines are Components/Actors, while the sequence messages are Functional or Component Exchanges;

– Interface Scenarios (ISs): the lifelines are also Components/ Actors but the sequence messages are Exchange Items.

We can find all three types of Scenarios at the System Analysis level in the Activity Explorer.

Figure 4.70. *Scenario diagrams at the System level*

NOTE (Arcadia Rule).– A Scenario describes the behavior of the System in the context of a particular Capability. Even if we do not wish to use this concept, Capella automatically creates a Capability the first time a Scenario is created, unless of course Capabilities already exist. In this case, Capella asks to choose one Capability to attach the new Scenario.

Let us start with the simplest Scenario type: the Functional Scenario.

We start by creating as an example a Scenario involving the Functional Chain of acquisition. We are therefore going to attach it to the Capability "Produce Weather Data". The Functional Scenario is a type of chronological System Data Flow Blank. The Functions are represented by vertical lines (instead of rectangles), and the Functional Exchanges are represented by horizontal arrows ordered sequentially from top to bottom.

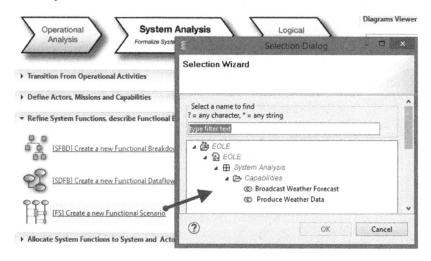

Figure 4.71. *Creating a Functional Scenario diagram*

NOTE.– Functional Scenario diagrams are given a name by default like: [FS] Scenario. Good practice involves adding the first letter of the level, and of course then giving a more meaningful name to the Scenario, such as [SFS] Acquisition Scenario.

To insert the Functions that we are interested in, we can drag and drop them from the *Project Explorer*, or insert them using the *Insert/Remove Functions* button in the palette.

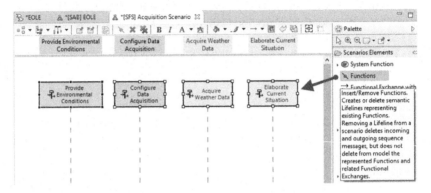

Figure 4.72. *Insertion of Functions in a Functional Scenario diagram. For a color version of the figure, see www.iste.co.uk/roques/arcadia.zip*

Next we create horizontal messages by selecting existing Functional Exchanges using the *Functional Exchange* tool in the palette.

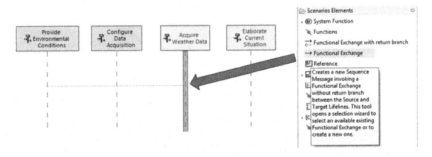

Figure 4.73. *Creating messages in a Functional Scenario diagram. For a color version of the figure, see www.iste.co.uk/roques/arcadia.zip*

Capella only allows us to select the Functional Exchanges that already exist in the model. As a result, here it only proposes "environmental conditions".

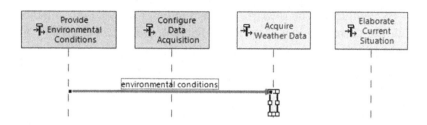

Figure 4.74. *First message created in the Functional Scenario diagram. For a color version of the figure, see www.iste.co.uk/roques/arcadia.zip*

NOTE.– Scenario diagrams in Capella are very similar to the UML/SysML sequence diagrams [CAS 18]. We can therefore create messages with return, "synchronous/asynchronous" types, etc., and use Combined Fragments, duration constraints, etc. We shall illustrate most of these options in examples later in the book at different levels of engineering. The property sheet of a message is provided in Figure 4.75.

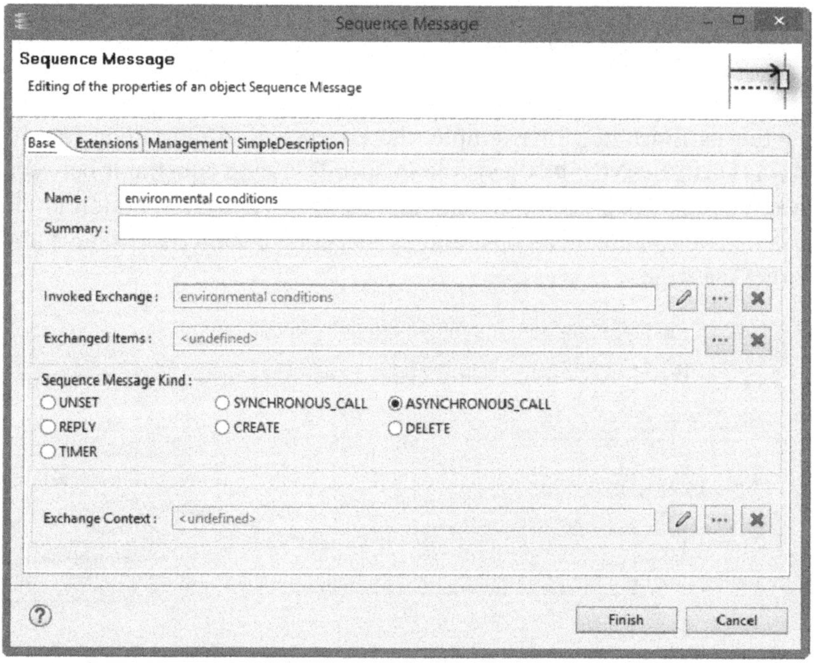

Figure 4.75. *Property sheet of a message*

By completing the scenario diagram in order to make it compatible with the corresponding Data Flow diagram, we obtain the following diagram.

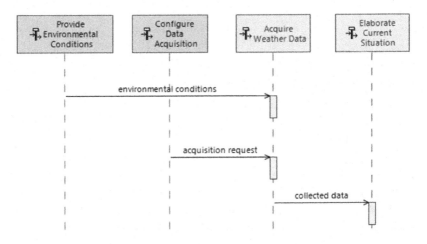

Figure 4.76. *Completed Functional Scenario diagram. For a color version of the figure, see www.iste.co.uk/roques/arcadia.zip*

Let us illustrate, for example, the concept of duration constraints. As in UML/SysML, it is possible to specify a time constraint between two messages in a Scenario diagram. Using the *Duration* button in the palette, we can create a constraint by selecting a source message and a target message.

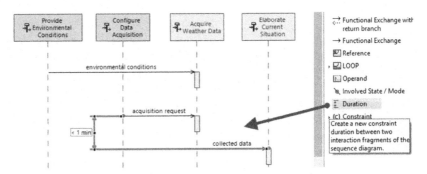

Figure 4.77. *Creation of a duration constraint. For a color version of the figure, see www.iste.co.uk/roques/arcadia.zip*

This constraint is a model element on its own and not only a graphical object. Its name appears in the *Project Explorer*, and its value in the diagram.

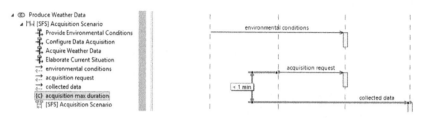

Figure 4.78. *Duration constraint in the explorer and the diagram. For a color version of the figure, see www.iste.co.uk/roques/arcadia.zip*

It is good practice to then rename the model element "Scenario" in the Project Explorer with the name of the diagram created, as shown in Figure 4.79. Note that the explorer shows the vertical lines, messages and constraints, which are all model elements in their own right, under the Scenario, which is itself under a Capability.

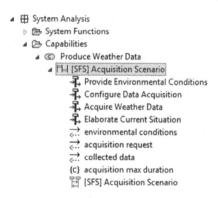

Figure 4.79. *Scenario and its model element in the Explorer*

We shall now create an ES diagram. This can of course be done by going through the *Activity Explorer*, as shown previously, and creating a new Scenario manually. Another option involves using an interesting Capability of the Capella tool, which can automatically initialize an ES from a Functional Scenario.

For this, we must position ourselves on the Scenario, either in the diagram that we have just created, or in the *Project Explorer*, and activate a contextual command with the right click: *Transitions – Function Scenario to Exchange Scenario Initialization*.

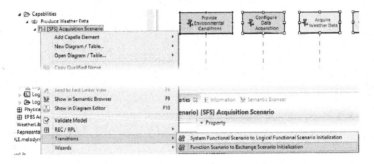

Figure 4.80. *Contextual transition of a Functional Scenario. For a color version of the figure, see www.iste.co.uk/roques/arcadia.zip*

The result of this initialization is a new ES, with the same horizontal messages, but only three vertical lines corresponding to the structural elements (here the System or the Actors) instead of the Functions.

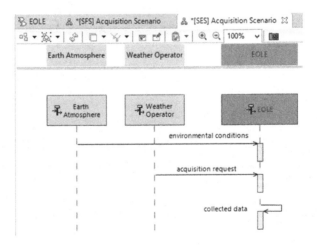

Figure 4.81. *Exchange Scenario obtained automatically by transition of a Functional Scenario. For a color version of the figure, see www.iste.co.uk/roques/arcadia.zip*

We just need to create the diagram, and rename the vertical lines in the Project Explorer (they are given the same name following the transition as those in the Functional Scenario). We can also show the Functions on the vertical lines, if we so desire. Capella helps the modeler and proposes only Functions allocated to the elements represented by vertical lines.

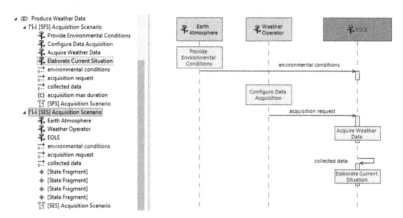

Figure 4.82. *Complete Exchange Scenario. For a color version of the figure, see www.iste.co.uk/roques/arcadia.zip*

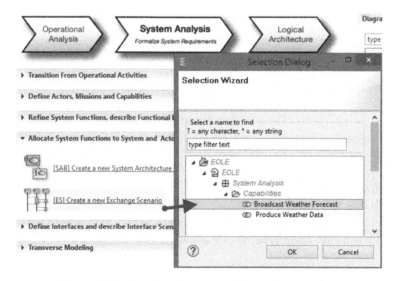

Figure 4.83. *Creation of a second Exchange Scenario*

We will now create a second diagram, this time via the *Activity Explorer*. This Scenario involves the other Capability of broadcasting weather forecast. It allows us to illustrate the concept of a fragment, which comes from UML/SysML.

NOTE.– The ES diagram at the SA level (SES) is the only one that is not empty. It always contains a vertical line representing the System as a "black box", in the same way that an Architecture diagram at the System level (SAB) always contains the System. However, most of the time a subset of Actors is enough for the Scenario involved. We will have to insert them into each Scenario diagram.

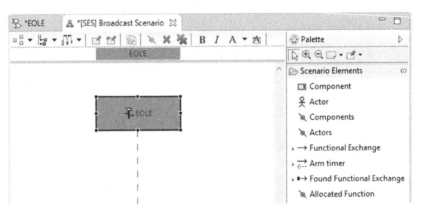

Figure 4.84. *System level Exchange Scenario after creation*

In this Scenario, first we will represent the nominal subscription sequence of the scientific user. To do this, we insert the Actor in question and select the relevant Functional Exchanges. By adding the corresponding Functions, we obtain the start of a Scenario, as shown in Figure 4.85.

We shall now describe a repetitive behavior: every day the System publishes information on the weather, which the user can receive as they have a subscription. For this, we shall use a Combined Fragment, which is of the *Loop* type, with a frequency of "every day".

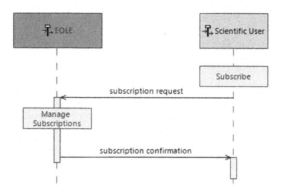

Figure 4.85. *Start of the "broadcast" Exchange Scenario. For a color version of the figure, see www.iste.co.uk/roques/arcadia.zip*

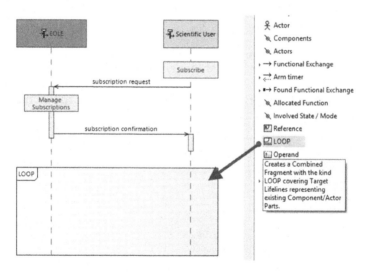

Figure 4.86. *Creating a Loop fragment. For a color version of the figure, see www.iste.co.uk/roques/arcadia.zip*

The fragment itself is a model element, with its own property sheet. Moreover, there is no standard graphical command that can be used to make it big or smaller horizontally: instead the semantic field *Covered Instance Roles* has to be modified. The vertical lines in the Scenarios are called Instance Roles in Capella (and Lifelines in UML/SysML).

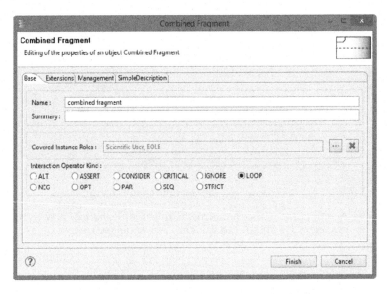

Figure 4.87. *Fragment property sheet*

We add the Actor "Broadcaster" into the Scenario and include it in the daily loop.

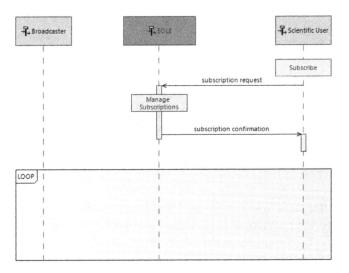

Figure 4.88. *Adding an Actor to the fragment. For a color version of the figure, see www.iste.co.uk/roques/arcadia.zip*

We can now complete the Scenario as shown in Figure 4.89.

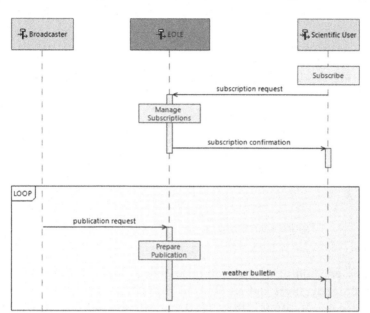

Figure 4.89. *Completed broadcast Exchange Scenario. For a color version of the figure, see www.iste.co.uk/roques/arcadia.zip*

NOTE.– The concept of Combined Fragment comes directly from UML/SysML. Each fragment contains an operator and can be split into operands. The main operands are:

– *loop*: the fragment can be executed several times, and the guard condition states the iteration;

– *opt*: optional. The fragment is only executed if the condition provided is true;

– *alt*: alternative operands. Only the operand containing the true condition is executed;

– *par*: parallel operands. All of the operands are executed in parallel.

In our example, in order to mark that the loop takes place every day, we must edit the unique operand contained in the *Loop* fragment.

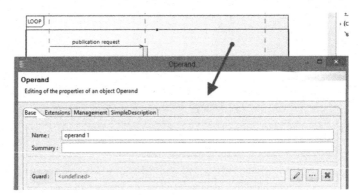

Figure 4.90. *Property sheet of a fragment operand*

The creation of a condition (also called Guard) is done through a new property sheet and an *Opaque Expression* type element. This is also a concept coming from UML/SysML that allows us to simply express a constraint in any given language. Do not forget to click on *LinkedText* when editing constraints.

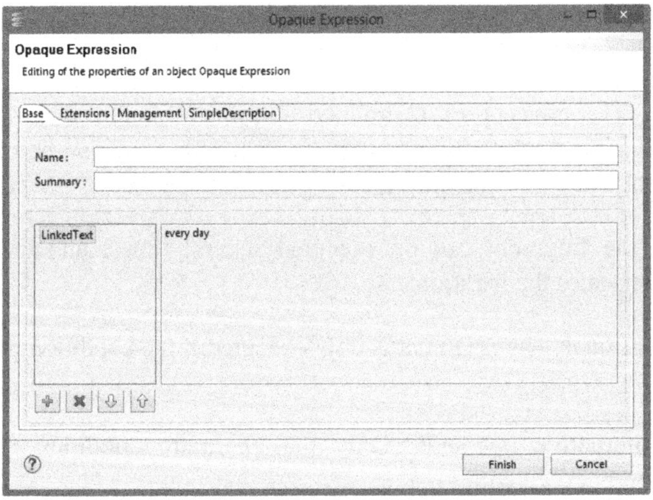

Figure 4.91. *Property sheet of an Opaque Expression*

The text of the condition is shown at the top left of the operand, in brackets.

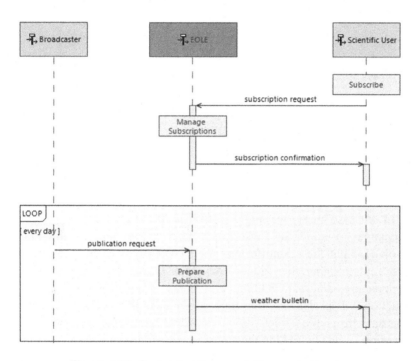

Figure 4.92. *Completed Fragment. For a color version of the figure, see www.iste.co.uk/roques/arcadia.zip*

Up to here we have used existing model elements to create vertical lines or horizontal messages in the Scenarios. It is perfectly possible to create these model elements directly from a scenario diagram. For example, we can add an Actor to the model by creating an *Instance Role* (instead of inserting an existing Actor).

Capella automatically creates the two model elements, the first as an Instance Role in the Scenario and the second as an Actor in the *Actors* folder.

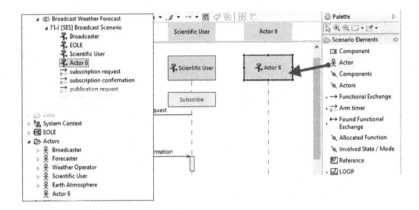

Figure 4.93. *Creation of an Actor from a Scenario. For a color version of the figure, see www.iste.co.uk/roques/arcadia.zip*

In our case study, we might instead need to create new Functional Exchanges to model the subscription process. For example, this might involve asking the scientific user for a card payment and waiting for their reply. Rather than going back to a Data Flow diagram, or an Architecture diagram, adding Functional Exchanges and possibly Functions, it is also possible here to do everything from a Scenario diagram. Instead of selecting an existing Exchange, we move into "creation" mode by ticking the *Create a new Functional Exchange* box.

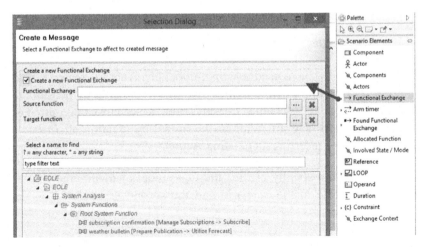

Figure 4.94. *Creation of a Functional Exchange from a Scenario*

To create a Functional Exchange we will need more than a name. Capella knows that a Functional Exchange always links two Functions. We must therefore first fill the two fields *Source Function* and *Target Function*, and click on *OK*.

Here again, Capella helps the modeler: it knows the existing Functions that have already been allocated to the vertical lines between which we want to create a message. In our example, the two Functions are "Utilize Forecast" and "Subscribe" for the scientific user, who is the receiver of the message. For the Source Function, it is the four EOLE Functions. Of course, we have chosen the Function "Manage Subscriptions".

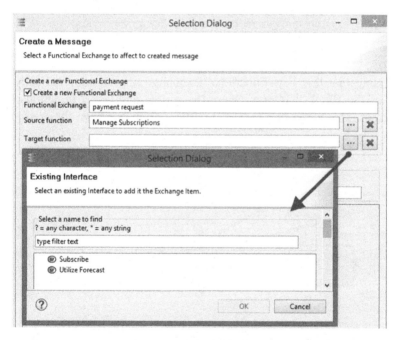

Figure 4.95. *Choice of Target and Source Functions during creation of a Functional Exchange from a Scenario*

With this simple maneuver, the modeler has not only created a message in the Scenario, but also a new Functional Exchange in the model.

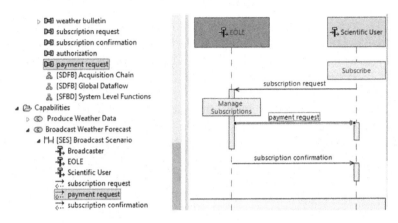

Figure 4.96. *Creation of a Functional Exchange from a message in a Scenario. For a color version of the figure, see www.iste.co.uk/roques/arcadia.zip*

Note that this new Functional Exchange appears automatically in all of the Blank diagrams where the source and target Functions are present. This is the case for the [SDFB] global data flow, for example.

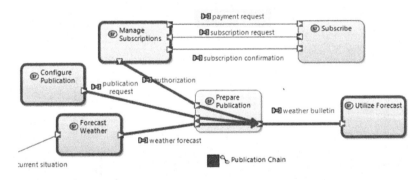

Figure 4.97. *Automatic adding of the Functional Exchange in an SDFB. For a color version of the figure, see www.iste.co.uk/roques/arcadia.zip*

This is also the case for the Architecture diagram (SAB), but here we can see that the new Functional Exchange still needs to be allocated to a Component Exchange. We can add it to an existing Component Exchange, typically here "secure Internet", or consider creating a new one.

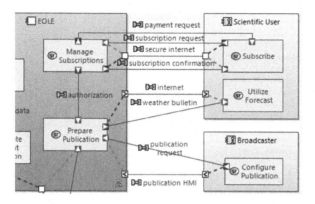

Figure 4.98. *Automatic adding of the Functional Exchange in an SAB. For a color version of the figure, see www.iste.co.uk/roques/arcadia.zip*

To finish off this topic, we will demonstrate that it is even possible to create new Functions from a Scenario diagram.

In the previous step, during the creation of the "payment request" message, instead of selecting one of the existing Functions of the Actor, we will create a new one, by simply writing a Function name in the corresponding field.

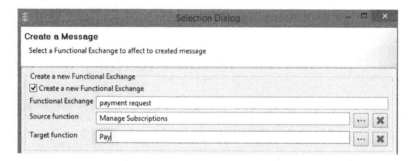

Figure 4.99. *Creation of a Target Function during creation of a Functional Exchange from a Scenario*

We can see that Capella has not only created a message in the Scenario and a Functional Exchange in the model, but has also created a new Function.

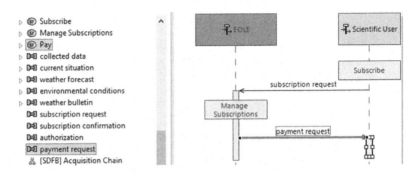

Figure 4.100. *Result of the creation of a Target Function during creation of a Functional Exchange from a Scenario. For a color version of the figure, see www.iste.co.uk/roques/arcadia.zip*

This new Function can immediately be used to appear on the vertical line to which it is allocated, i.e. the scientific user.

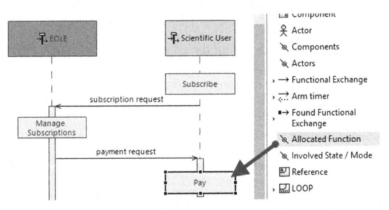

Figure 4.101. *Adding the new Target Function to the Scenario. For a color version of the figure, see www.iste.co.uk/roques/arcadia.zip*

NOTE.– This ability to create Actors, Functional Exchanges and even Functions from Scenarios is very interesting. Scenario diagrams are often used in the area of telecommunication for example, but also by many people who find it more instinctive and easier to specify and design a System from real stories (Scenarios). This was indeed the objective of Jacobson's Use Cases technique, which is integrated in UML/SysML [CAS 18].

4.8. Modes and States at the System level

Mode and State diagrams are graphical representations of State Machines inspired from UML/SysML.

Arcadia allows a State Machine to be associated with any structural element:

– Entity/Operational Actor;

– System/Actor;

– Logical Component/Logical Actor;

– Physical Component/Physical Actor.

The expected behavior of the System is often specified as a State Machine, particularly if the System must react to events coming from Actors in a set order. An Operational Entity can have a State Machine if it is standardized "business" knowledge for example, which could later be of consequence for our System under study. Some Physical Components often need State Machines to indicate under which States their Functions are available. For example, in our case study, at the Physical level, the helium balloon does not have the same behavior at ground level as in the air, out of reach, etc.

Let us quickly present the main concepts used. First the notion of State or Mode. In UML/SysML, a State represents a situation during the lifetime of a block during which:

– it satisfies a certain condition;

– it executes a certain behavior;

– or it expects a certain event.

NOTE.– Arcadia proposes two similar concepts: *State* and *Mode*. The use of one or the other is a methodological choice in the context of the project or the company. A fairly widespread difference among system engineers involves considering that the System Mode depends on a choice, often of an operator, while the State is the result of that which has happened to the System. In this way, we would talk of a manual mode, a semiautomatic mode, but of a default state. Unfortunately, there is no normalized definition of these two concepts. We therefore have to choose whichever word is the most relevant for our context and will connect most with the readers of the model. The two concepts cannot be mixed together in the same diagram.

States (or Modes) are linked together by Transitions. A Transition describes the reaction of a structural element when an event takes place (the element usually changes State as a result, but this is not always the case). A transition contains a source State, a Trigger and a target State. It can also include a Guard Condition as well as an Effect.

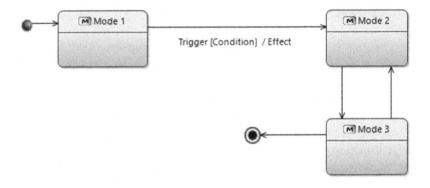

Figure 4.102. *Basic notation of Mode and State diagram (MSM)*

On top of the succession of "normal" States corresponding to the life cycle of a structural element, the State diagram also contains two pseudo-states:

– the initial State of the State diagram corresponds to the creation of the element;

– the final State of the State diagram corresponds to the destruction of the element.

In particular, this allows us to model the issue of managing the end of the life cycle for a System or a Component.

In our case study, we are going to associate a simple Mode machine with the EOLE System. To do this, we go back to the *Activity Explorer* and into the section "Transverse Modeling", to create a Mode State Machine (MSM) diagram.

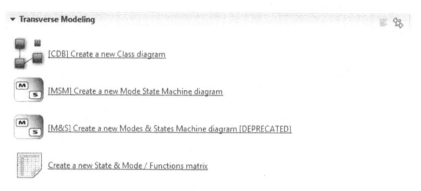

Figure 4.103. *Creation of a Mode State Machine (MSM) diagram*

NOTE.– Capella 1.1 proposes two versions of the Mode and State diagram. This is a very powerful and complex diagram in UML/SysML, and is still evolving in Capella. Capella 1.1 has notably added the possibility of creating concurrent regions (to represent parallelism between States), which was not possible in previous versions. For compatibility reasons, the old and new diagrams exist alongside each other for the moment.

When we ask for the creation of a MSM, Capella opens a selection window, proposing all of the structural elements of the Arcadia level involved, which in this case are the System and the Actors. We choose the EOLE system.

We shall not go into detail regarding all of the concepts offered in this type of diagram, and instead focus on only the most important ones. First, we create three Modes for the System: *Inactive*, *Operational* and *Acquisition*, and Transitions between these Modes. *Inactive* is the initial Mode.

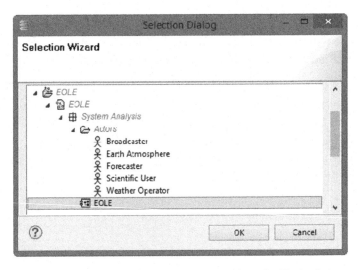

Figure 4.104. *Selection window for the creation of a Mode diagram*

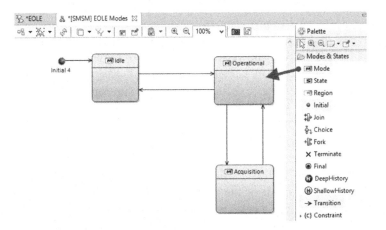

Figure 4.105. *Start of the Mode diagram*

We have hidden the names of the regions by activating the *Hide Region names* filter on the diagram. We could also hide the name of the initial pseudo-state by selecting it, and then applying the *Hide label* command. Let us stop for a moment on the concept of Mode, and open its property sheet. It contains a certain number of specific fields, with concepts that come from UML/SysML:

– Entry: An entry Effect represents an Effect that is executed each time the Mode/State is entered into. This allows us to factorize a same Effect that is set off by all of the transitions that enter into the Mode/State.

– Do activity: In opposition to Effects that are instantaneous, durable activities have a duration, can be interrupted and are always associated with Modes/States.

– Exit: An exit Effect represents an Effect that is executed every time that the Mode/State is exited. This allows us to factorize a same Effect that is set off by all of the transitions that exit the Mode/State.

The last field, however, called *Operational Activities/Functions* is specific to Arcadia and does not come from UML/SysML. It allows us to declare which Functions (or Activities at the Operational level) are available in the Mode in question.

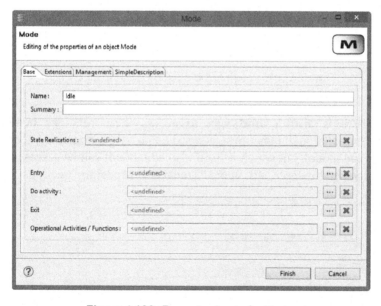

Figure 4.106. *Property sheet of a Mode*

Note that this relation is also visible in the Property sheet of Functions. We can therefore indicate, for example, that the Function

"Acquire Weather Data" is available in the "Acquisition" mode. The relation is now in the model, and will be shown in the property sheet of the "Acquisition" Mode next time that it is opened.

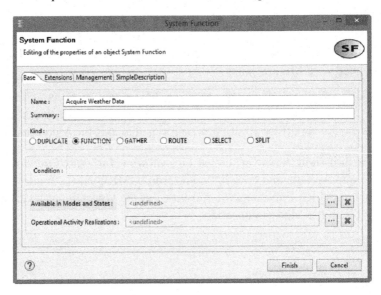

Figure 4.107. *Return to the property sheet of a Function*

There is also a third way to access these relations between Modes/States and Functions: a matrix that is generated by Capella from the model, but which is itself also editable. It can be accessed via the *Activity Explorer*, still in the "Transverse Modeling" section.

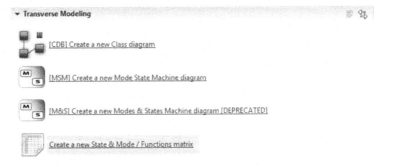

Figure 4.108. *Creation of a Mode/Functions matrix*

This matrix contains the structural elements in lines, with their possible Modes and States. It places the Functions in the columns, as well as the Functional Chains and the Capabilities. The availability relation is marked by an "X".

Figure 4.109. *Example of a Mode/Functions matrix*

In this way, it is possible to quickly complete these availability relations by simply adding "X"'s to the relevant cells. Note that if a Functional Chain is declared to be available in a certain Mode or State, Capella verifies that all of the Functions involved in the Chain are also declared available in the same Mode or State, issuing a warning if this is not the case, as shown Figure 4.110.

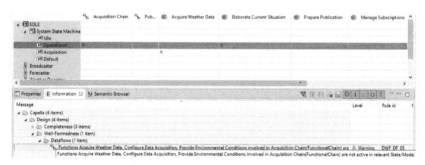

Figure 4.110. *Mode/Functions and Functional Chain incoherence warning*

NOTE.– Capella proposes various matrices at all levels of Arcadia. Notably, we can mention realization matrices between levels, which are very practical for rapidly declaring a large number of traceability relations, typically in the context of a bottom-up modeling process. Allocation matrices also present the advantage of providing a synthetic view of the allocation of Functions to structural elements. Careful though, as editing these allocation matrices modifies the model and the corresponding Architecture diagrams as a result.

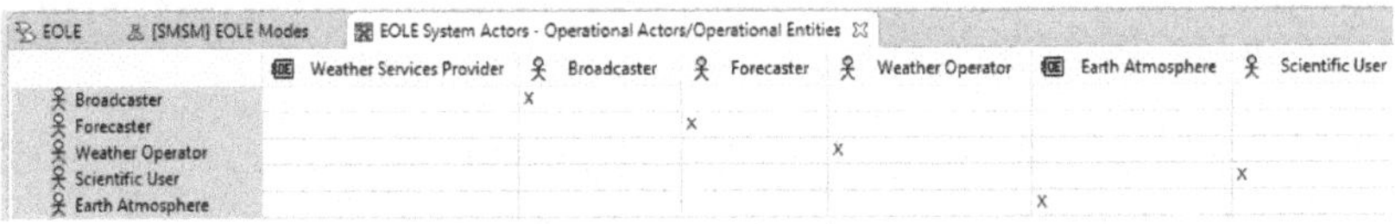

Figure 4.111. *Example of an Operational Entities/System Actors matrix*

In the previous matrix, we can immediately see that the Operational Entity called "Weather Services Provider" is not realized by a System level Actor, while all the other operational structural elements are realized. Remember that this choice was made knowingly in our case study, and we accept the due warning.

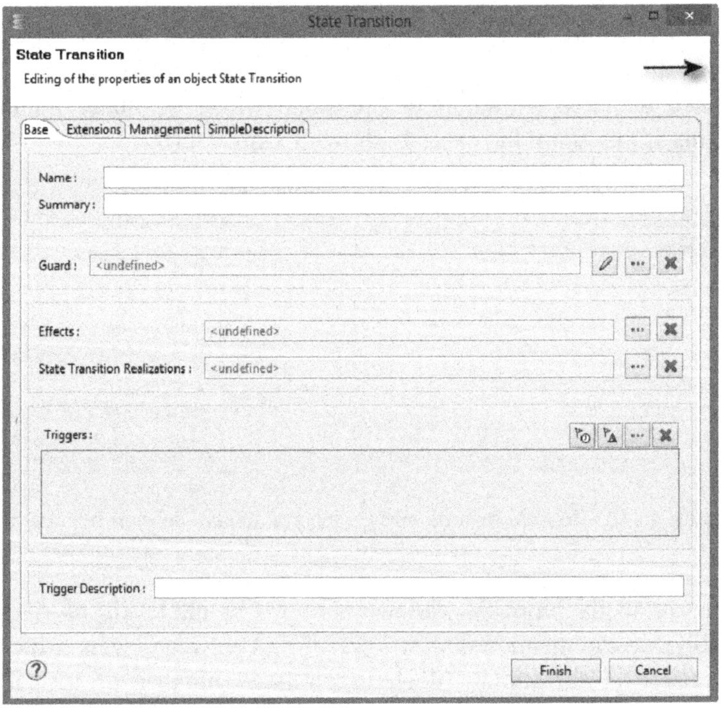

Figure 4.112. *Property sheet of a transition*

Let us go back now to the concept of transition between Modes and States. Remember that a transition describes the reaction of a structural element when an event takes place. It has a source State, a Trigger and a target State. It can also contain a Guard Condition and an Effect, as shown on figure 4.112.

Let us start with the Trigger. In the current version of Capella, it can be named by free text in the "Trigger Description" field. It is good practice to use an existing model element, such as a Functional Exchange, for example, in the *Triggers* field. In our example, let us express the fact that the system goes from the "Operational" mode to the "Acquisition" mode with each "acquisition request". To do this, we must choose the Functional Exchange in the selection window of the *Triggers* field.

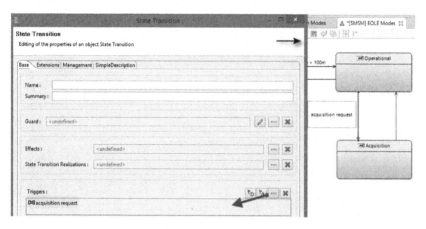

Figure 4.113. *Choice of a Trigger among the existing model elements*

NOTE.– Capella is meant to be very close to UML/SysML with regard to the State diagram. A trigger can therefore also be a Time Event or a Change Event. A Time Event is modeled using either the keyword "*after*", followed by an expression that represents duration, counted from the entrance into the current State, or the keyword "*at*", followed by an expression that represents an absolute time. Change Events are modeled using the keyword "*when*", followed by a Boolean expression, in which the passing from false to true sets off the transition.

For example, here we shall use the notion of Change Event to express the fact that the EOLE system moves into "Operational" mode as soon as the altitude of the balloon is greater than 100 m. This is obviously a simplification for teaching purposes....

To create a Change Event, we must click on the flag with a triangle in the *Triggers* field (the clock on the side lets us create a Time Event). A property sheet then opens, allowing us to edit the name and the expression of the Change Event.

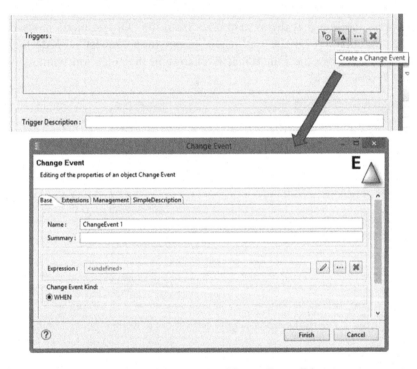

Figure 4.114. *Creation of a Change Event Trigger*

We edit the expression field by using the name of the associated constraint, and we name the event in order to be able to find it within the Project Explorer.

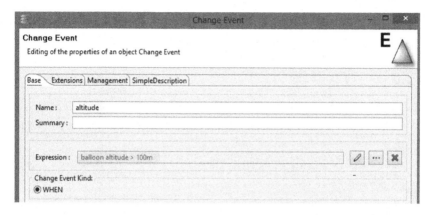

Figure 4.115. *Finalization of a Change Event Trigger*

The Mode and State diagram is updated, and the keyword *WHEN* appears automatically in front of the constraint.

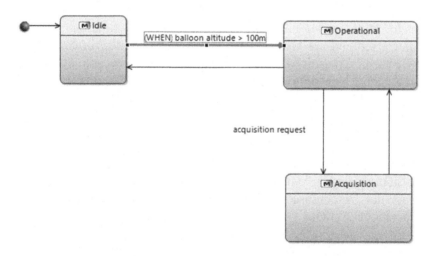

Figure 4.116. *Follow-up of the System Mode and State diagram. For a color version of the figure, see www.iste.co.uk/roques/arcadia.zip*

To complete this diagram, we shall express the fact that the "Acquisition" Mode effectively corresponds to the execution of the corresponding Function, and not only to its availability. To do this, we open the property sheet of the "Acquisition" Mode and choose the function "Acquire Weather Data" in the *Do activity* field.

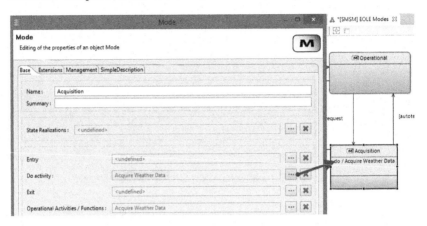

Figure 4.117. *Example of a durable activity in a Mode or State*

In UML/SysML, durable activities have a duration, can be interrupted and are always associated with the States, in contrast to Effects on Transitions. The normal end of a finite activity, called completion transition (or automatic transition), is represented in UML/SysML without an event or keyword. In our case study, the transition from "Acquisition" to "Operational" Mode is a good example.

NOTE.– The word "activity" used previously comes from UML/SysML vocabulary, and more or less represents a treatment or transformation. It must not be confused with the more specific concept of Arcadia Operational Activity.

Let us go back to the other concepts that are available in a transition, starting with the notion of Condition or Guard. In UML/SysML, a guard condition is a Boolean expression that must be true when the event takes place for the transition to be triggered. It is written between brackets. It can involve the values of the block in question, as well as the parameters of the trigger. Several transitions starting from the same source State with the same event must have different guard conditions in order to guarantee the determinism of the behavior.

We are going to add a Guard to our State diagram. We assume that at the end of acquisition, an autotest takes place. If this autotest is OK, the system returns to the "Operational" Mode. However, if the autotest fails, the system enters a new Mode called "Fault". We just need to edit the Guard field of the existing completion transition and add a Boolean expression.

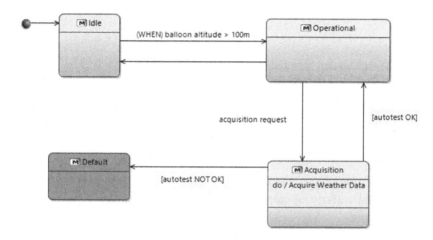

Figure 4.118. *Adding conditions to the System Mode and State diagram. For a color version of the figure, see www.iste.co.uk/roques/arcadia.zip*

We must now discuss the concept of Effect in order to complete our overview of the modeling concepts linked to the notion of Transition. In UML/SysML, a Transition can specify an optional behavior carried out by the structural element when the Transition is triggered. This behavior is called "Effect": this can be a simple action or sequence of actions (a UML action can represent the updating of a value, an operation call, as well as the sending of a signal to another element). Execution of the Effect is unitary and no other additional events can be treated while it is running.

With Capella 1.1, the concept of Effect can only be linked to the initializing of the execution of a Function of the structural element involved. In our example, instead of placing the function "Acquire Weather Data" in the *Do activity* field, we can consider its launching to be the transition Effect triggered by the acquisition request.

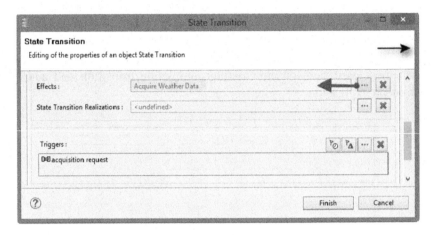

Figure 4.119. *Adding an Effect to a transition*

These two ways of modeling are quite similar, although the notion of durable activity is more in line with the completion transitions of our example.

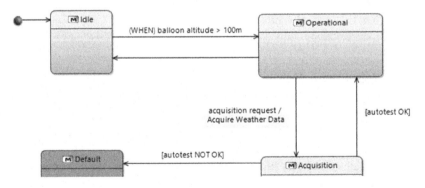

Figure 4.120. *Adding an Effect to the System Mode and State diagram*

To conclude this section on the Mode and State diagram, it must be added that Modes/States can also be made to appear in ES diagrams.

Indeed, it can be useful to specify the Mode of the different structural elements at the start of the Scenario, at the end, or at intermediate stages. This is particularly interesting when the Scenario has been described for the purpose of testing, and allows specification of preconditions, postconditions, etc., that the tester will have to verify. In our example with a nominal acquisition Scenario, the System must be in the "Operational" Mode for the Scenario to make sense. The System then goes into "Acquisition" Mode, and then back into "Operational" Mode.

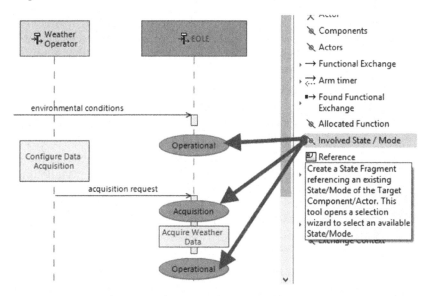

Figure 4.121. *Adding System Modes and States to the Scenario diagram. For a color version of the figure, see www.iste.co.uk/roques/arcadia.zip*

4.9. Data modeling at the System level

An important part of system engineering involves ensuring coherence between the data managed in the system and the data exchanged with external actors. In order to unambiguously describe these exchanges, the data, information, matter flow, etc., must be formalized. Beyond this description, an important engineering task involves avoiding multiple definitions for a single piece of data in different areas of the system. Hence, the need to declare that several exchanges should carry the same type of data, without having to redefine the shared data for each exchange.

It is in this context that Capella provides advanced mechanisms for modeling data structures with the desired level of precision, and links them to Functional Exchanges, Function or Component Ports, Interfaces, etc.

NOTE (Arcadia Rule).– It must be noted that this data modeling is transverse to all levels of Arcadia. In particular, a Type defined at the System Analysis level can be used at all of the lower levels, down to the Physical Architecture level. It is therefore not necessary to carry out a "transition" of the definitions of Types, as is done for Functions or Actors, for example. The opposite is not true: a Type defined at a given Arcadia level cannot be used at higher levels.

Definitions of Exchange Items (EIs), Classes, Types, etc., are mainly established in Capella through diagrams called Class Diagram Blanks. These CDB are available at every level of abstraction in Arcadia and are placed under the theme of "Transverse Modeling" (just like Mode and State diagrams).

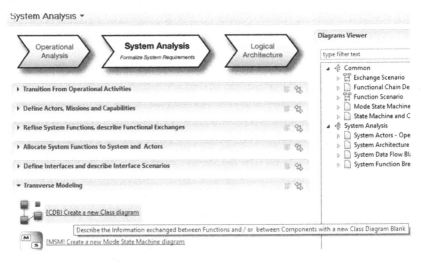

Figure 4.122. *Creation of a Class diagram*

There are two main categories of concepts in this type of diagram:

– Communication elements: EIs and Interfaces;

– Type definitions: basic Types, Classes, relations between Classes.

These two categories of concepts are taken into account in a division of the CDB's palette into two different groups.

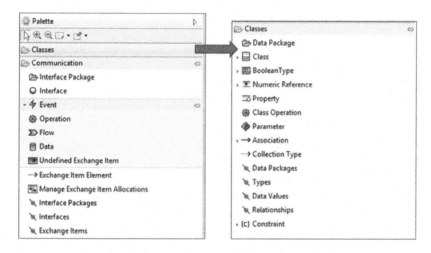

Figure 4.123. *Palette of the Class diagram (CDB)*

NOTE.– The Class diagram palette is very comprehensive, and we most likely will not need to use all of the concepts on offer in any of our projects. Moreover, the property sheets of these model elements are also very extensive, allowing those who wish to develop their formalizations in great depth. Do not forget to adapt your modeling effort to your objectives, without getting distracted by all of the options provided by Arcadia and Capella....

Let us start by considering the communication elements and, in particular, the EIs. An EI has a name and a communication mechanism. It defines a coherent set of data in terms of use in a certain context, of a communication principle, as well as of non-functional properties and of transport simultaneity.

There are four predefined communication mechanisms in ARCADIA:

– EVENT: asynchronous mechanism where an event is sent by an element and received by one or several others;

– FLOW: flow of matter, energy, etc. or data;

– OPERATION: process carried out by an element and invoked by another;

– SHARED DATA: data modified by an element and read by others.

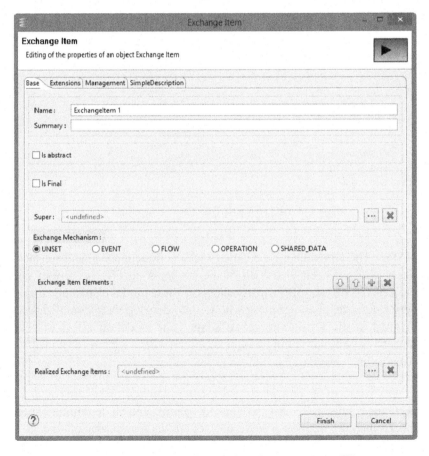

Figure 4.124. *Property sheet of an Exchange Item (EI)*

In the first stages of the engineering process, the communication mechanism applied to a given EI might not be known or decided upon. In such a case, the *UNSET* "joker" could be used. The choice of communication mechanism can be refined later using the property sheet of the EI.

Each EI refers to one or several Types of data, via the *EI Elements*. We shall return to this a bit later.

We shall look now at the definitions of the Types proposed by Capella: Classes, Structured Types, Simple Types. The vocabulary used comes from UML, and the very name of the "Class diagram" is a direct reference to it.

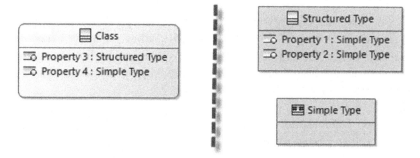

Figure 4.125. *Definitions of Types in Capella. For a color version of the figure, see www.iste.co.uk/roques/arcadia.zip*

The simple Types predefined by Capella are as follows: BooleanType, Enumeration, NumericType, StringType and PhysicalQuantity. Careful, BooleanLiteral and EnumerationLiteral help define Boolean Type and Enumeration, while Unit helps to define PhysicalQuantity.

Simple types cannot have properties. If we want to define Structured Types, the Class button in the palette must be used, and then the Class must be specified as primitive (tick the box *Is Primitive*). The other "Primitive" Classes then play the role of structured Types, and can in turn type the properties of the "true" Classes.

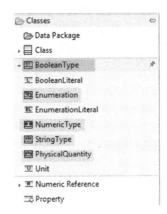

Figure 4.126. *The basic Types predefined by Capella*

To make the analogy with UML, the concept of Primitive Class corresponds to that of *DataType* in UML, whose instances have no identity, unlike for Classes. Classes in Capella can be linked together through associations, aggregations, compositions or generalizations, as in UML [ROQ 04].

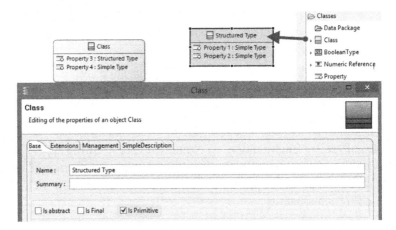

Figure 4.127. *Creation of a Structured Type with Capella. For a color version of the figure, see www.iste.co.uk/roques/arcadia.zip*

We can now go back to the concept of EI Element, which links EIs to Classes and Types.

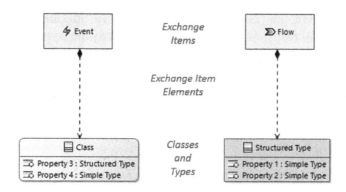

Figure 4.128. *Relations between EI and Types in Capella. For a color version of the figure, see www.iste.co.uk/roques/arcadia.zip*

It must be noted that the EI Element is itself a model element, with its own property sheet, which is also quite complex (but here again, there is no need to use all of it…).

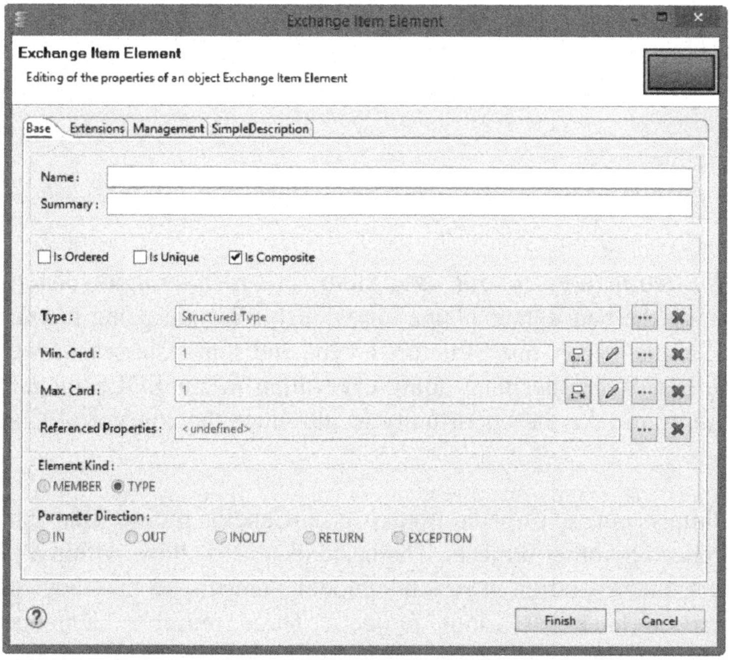

Figure 4.129. *Property sheet of an Exchange Item Element*

By default, the *Is Composite* box is ticked, meaning the EI in question will really contain the elements typed by the target Type. The default cardinality is exactly 1, but the fields *Min. Card* and *Max Card* allow us to specify an optionality (min = 0), or on the contrary, a multiplicity (max > 1). The notion of PARAMETER is particularly useful for EIs for which the exchange mechanism is OPERATION.

The links between the EI and the EI Elements are shown in the property sheet of the EI.

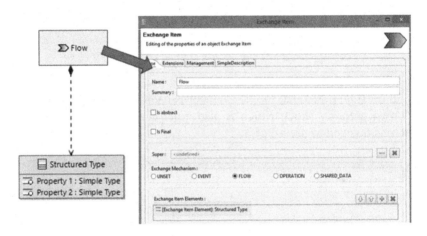

Figure 4.130. *Return to the property sheet of an Exchange Item*

We return now to our case study in order to more concretely illustrate the concepts explained previously. We are going to create a few Simple Types, one Structured Type and some Classes, as well as some EIs. But rather than doing everything in our EOLE model, we are going to take the opportunity to introduce the concept of Capella library.

Simply put, a Capella library is a Capella project that can be referenced by other projects. The basic idea is to allow, within a given project, the separation of reusable model elements, so that they can be referenced later in various projects. These reusable elements are mainly definitions of Types and Classes of the domain, as well as basic Physical Components unique to a given domain. This list is not restrictive; however, a library can contain the same model elements and the same Arcadia levels as classical projects.

To create a Capella library, there is a specific command that must be applied: *File – New – Capella Library*. Note that a project cannot be transformed into a library in version 1.1 of Capella.

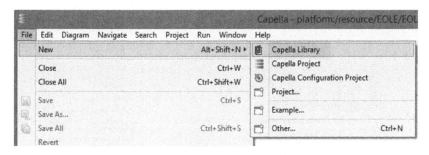

Figure 4.131. *Creating a Capella library*

As stated, the model thus created is entirely similar to a classical Capella model, apart from the different icons in front of the project and model root. As for any Capella project, we could have unticked the Operational Analysis and EPBS levels.

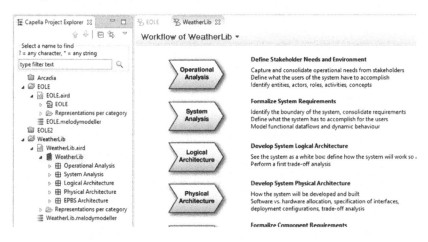

Figure 4.132. *Result of the creation of a Capella library*

We have seen that Type definitions can be used at the level at which they were declared, as well as at all lower levels. It is therefore good practice to declare the reusable Types of the domain at the highest Arcadia level, which is Operational Analysis. Moreover, it can noted that by default Capella proposes a certain number of basic Types at the System level in a subfolder called *Predefined Types* located in the folder called *Data*. In light of the comment made above, we shall move the folder to the Operational level.

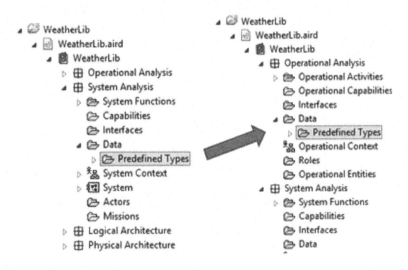

Figure 4.133. *File reorganization in the Explorer*

It must be noted that Capella does not usually leave much room for reorganizing folders (called "packages") in the *Project Explorer*, in an attempt to maintain model coherence. It would indeed be very dangerous to be able to move Logical Components to other levels, etc. However, definitions of Types, Classes, EIs, etc., can be easily reorganized if necessary, for example by sliding-moving folders in the Project Explorer.

We shall now create a new subfolder in the predefined *Data* package, which we call "Domain Types" using the contextual command *Add Capella Element–Data Pkg*. It is in this subfolder that we place the Class diagram (CDB) through the contextual menu.

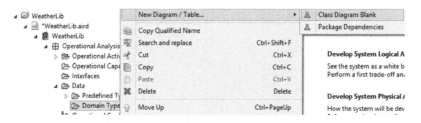

Figure 4.134. *Creation of packages and diagrams in the explorer*

In this Class diagram, we are going to create:

– Two Units: Celsius and hectoPascal;

– Two Physical Quantities: Temperature_C, Pressure_hPa;

– Two Numeric Types: Hour and Minute;

– One Structured Type: Timestamp.

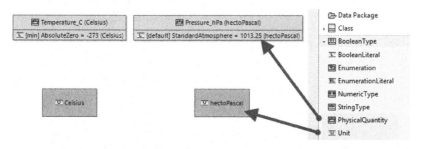

Figure 4.135. *Creation of Units and Physical Quantities. For a color version of the figure, see www.iste.co.uk/roques/arcadia.zip*

Note the extensiveness of the basic Type property sheet, and even of the Literal Values.

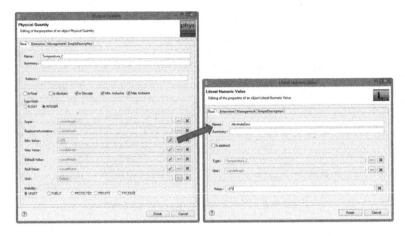

Figure 4.136. *Property sheet of a Physical Quantity*

Numeric Types have the same property sheet as Physical Quantities, except for the missing Unit field. To create a Structured Type, as explained before, we must use the concept of Class, and tick *Is Primitive*. The two properties in the Class are then added using the palette (*Property*).

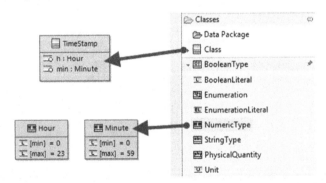

Figure 4.137. *Creation of a Structured Type in the library. For a color version of the figure, see www.iste.co.uk/roques/arcadia.zip*

We shall now return to our EOLE project and create some EIs to describe the three functional flows of the acquisition Chain. We shall create a flow of air particles coming from the atmosphere, and exchanges of unspecified mechanism for the acquisition request and for the measurement of temperature and pressure.

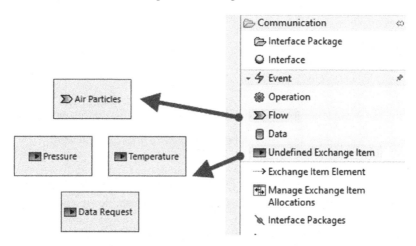

Figure 4.138. *Creating Exchange Items in the EOLE project. For a color version of the figure, see www.iste.co.uk/roques/arcadia.zip*

We must now link these EIs to Classes or Types. However, to do this, we must have access to Types defined in the domain library. This requires referencing the library in our project. Capella allows us do this by right clicking on the ".aird" file in the *Project Explorer*.

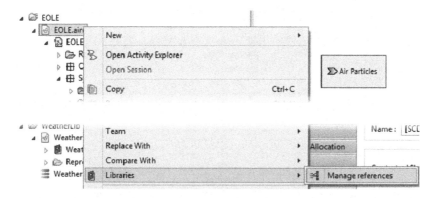

Figure 4.139. *Referencing a library in a project*

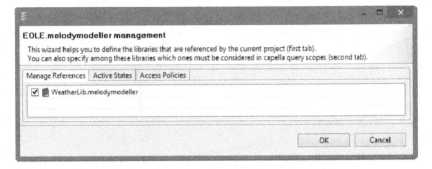

Figure 4.140. *Referencing a library in a project (continued)*

The library becomes visible inside the project, and all of the model elements that are defined within it are accessible if the different Arcadia levels are compatible.

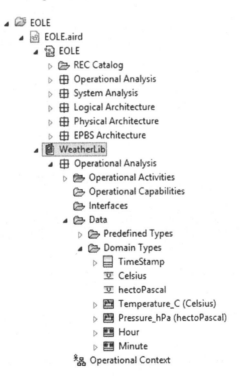

Figure 4.141. *Referencing a library in a project (end)*

We can now use the Types of the domain library, such as the Simple Types "Temperature_C" and "Pressure_hPa", as well as the Structured Type "Timestamp" for our new Class "DataRequest". To insert the library Types into our diagram, the command *Insert/Remove Types* from the palette is used. We now not only have access to the Types defined in the EOLE model, but also those from the referenced library, at the Operational and System levels.

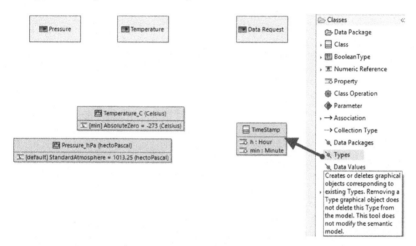

Figure 4.142. *Insertion of library Types into the project CDB. For a color version of the figure, see www.iste.co.uk/roques/arcadia.zip*

The class "DataRequest" will have two Timestamp type properties, called "requestTime" and "captureTime", the latter of which is optional. The capture time only needs to be stated if capture is performed on demand, otherwise it takes place at a fixed time. The property sheet of a Class Property allows specification of min and max cardinalities (1 by default). By moving the min cardinality from 1 to 0, we are specifying an optional Property.

NOTE.– Once again, note the breadth of this property sheet, which allows us to specify a default value, a null value, etc., as well as characteristics that are close to object programming language, such as *Is Static*, *Is abstract* or *Visibility*. Because of the *Capella Studio* environment, it is indeed possible to develop code generators from the information contained in a Capella model, even if this is not the main objective of this type of system modeling.

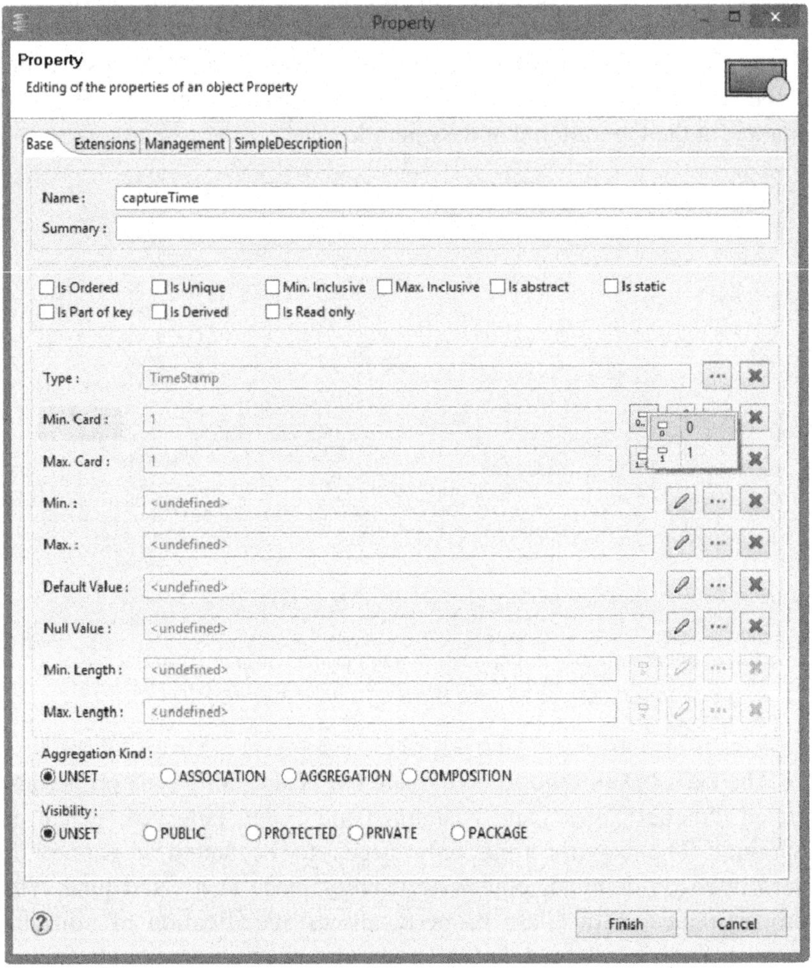

Figure 4.143. *Property sheet of a Class Property*

We must now link our EIs to Types and Classes that define their content through several EI Elements. This can be done either graphically in the Class diagram, or through the property sheet of the EI.

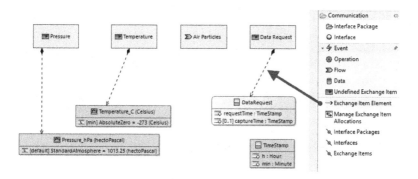

Figure 4.144. *Finalizing the Class diagram. For a color version of the figure, see www.iste.co.uk/roques/arcadia.zip*

The last step of our little exercise is to link the Functional Exchanges and the EIs. The simplest way to do this is to select the Functional Exchanges involved in a diagram or the *Project Explorer* and to open their property sheet. Going back to the complete SAB for example, we double-click on the "acquisition request" FE. The first field of the sheet is called *Exchanged Items* and allows us to select the EIs that interest us.

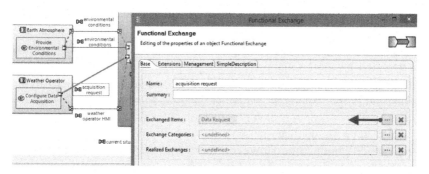

Figure 4.145. *Link between Functional Exchange and Exchange Item. For a color version of the figure, see www.iste.co.uk/roques/arcadia.zip*

We thus associate the "Data Request" EI with the "acquisition request" FE, the "Air Particles" EI with the "environmental conditions" FE and the two "Pressure" and "Temperature" EIs with the "collected data" FE. The Architecture diagram itself is not modified, but all of the chain of linked concepts can be seen in the *Semantic Browser*.

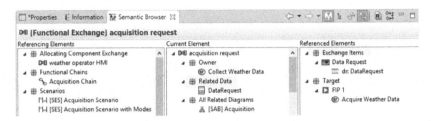

Figure 4.146. *Links between concepts seen in the Semantic Browser. For a color version of the figure, see www.iste.co.uk/roques/arcadia.zip*

We have thus allocated EIs to Functional Exchanges, but Arcadia actually recommends allocating EIs to each Function Port in order to characterize the content that the Function could produce or could need.

NOTE.– At least one EI should be allocated to each Function Port. This EI could be shared between several Ports, and actually should be shared by the two Ports at the extremities of a Functional Exchange. If a Function Port has several EIs, then it should be specified on each Functional Exchange connected to it, which are the elements that are actually conveyed, which must be coherent with those of the Ports connected by the Exchange. Capella proposes a *Modeling Accelerator* to propagate the EIs of a Functional Exchange toward each of the Function Ports: *Propagate Exchange Items to Function Ports*.

We have stated that the Architecture Blank diagram (SAB) was unchanged graphically. However, there is a way of displaying the EIs in this type of diagram. To achieve this, we apply an additional filter: *Show Exchange Items on Functional Exchanges*. After a *Refresh* on the diagram (F5), we obtain the following figure, where the EIs appear in brackets, instead of the names of the Functional Exchange involved. This is finest level of detail that can be achieved in this type of diagram.

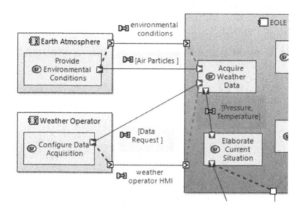

Figure 4.147. *Exchange Items instead of Functional Exchanges. For a color version of the figure, see www.iste.co.uk/roques/arcadia.zip*

In a similar fashion, let us now go back to the SAB showing the external exchanges, and apply the additional filter: *Show Exchange Items on Component Exchanges*. After a *Refresh* of the diagram (F5), we obtain the following figure, where the EI appear in parentheses after the name of the FE involved.

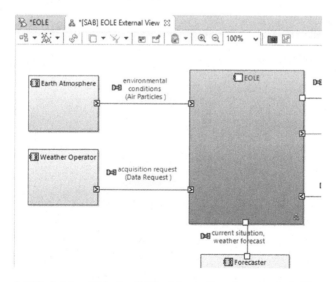

Figure 4.148. *Adding EI to the SAB of the external exchanges. For a color version of the figure, see www.iste.co.uk/roques/arcadia.zip*

Continuing on the subject of EIs, we must state that it is also possible to make them appear in scenarios, called Interface Scenarios (IS). Capella is even capable of automatically initializing an IS from an ES.

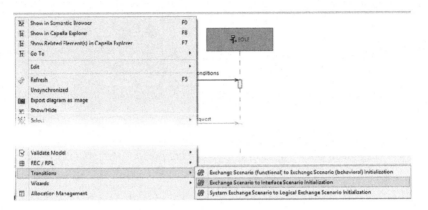

Figure 4.149. *Initializing an IS from an ES*

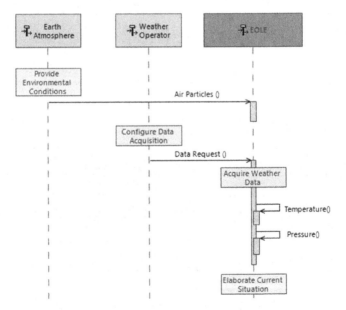

Figure 4.150. *Example of IS finalization from an ES. For a color version of the figure, see www.iste.co.uk/roques/arcadia.zip*

We go back to our "[SES] Acquisition scenario", and apply the command: *Transitions – Exchange Scenario to Interface Scenario Initialization* through the contextual menu. Capella will create a new Scenario, where the vertical lines and the Functions are preserved. All that is left to do is to add the horizontal messages, which represent EIs and no longer FEs, as is shown in Figure 4.150.

We could also have stated earlier in the process, from the SES onward, which EIs are carried by the messages. This is particularly interesting when a Functional Exchange contains several EIs: it allows us to choose which subset is present in the scenario involved.

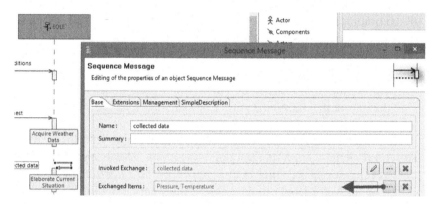

Figure 4.151. *Details on the EIs of a message in an ES*

With the right filter, the EIs can now be seen in the SES.

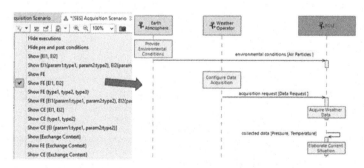

Figure 4.152. *Displaying the EIs of a message in an ES. For a color version of the figure, see www.iste.co.uk/roques/arcadia.zip*

Note that if we have associated EIs to messages from the SES onward, the transition of the ES to an IS preserves the EIs and automatically generates the Scenario, as shown in Figure 4.150.

To finish off on the subject of EIs, we can add that it is also possible to group them into Interfaces. Capella proposes this concept to any modelers who might want it, and it is very similar to the concept that exists in UML and in certain object-oriented programming languages.

NOTE (Arcadia Rule).– An Interface is a collection of EIs, semantically coherent, that allow two Components (and the System and the Actors), to communicate along a communication "contract" shared between them. At least one Interface should be allocated to each Component Port of a component to characterize the EIs that the component can produce or that it needs. An Interface can be shared by several Components, and in fact should be shared by the two Component Ports of the Components at the extremities of a Component Exchange.

Capella is able to automatically calculate the Interfaces of a structural element from its Function allocations. This is a sophisticated new accelerator called *Interfaces from Allocated Functions*. Let us try it first on an Actor from our case study: the weather operator.

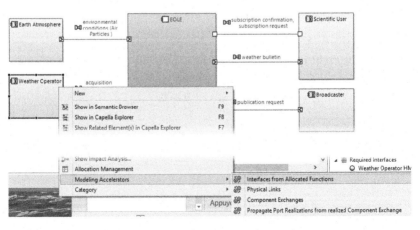

Figure 4.153. *Use of a new modeling accelerator. For a color version of the figure, see www.iste.co.uk/roques/arcadia.zip*

Capella has created an Interface called "Weather Operator HMI" in the Interfaces package, from the name of the Component Exchange. This Interface contains a reference to the EI "Data Request", which leaves the weather operator to go toward EOLE.

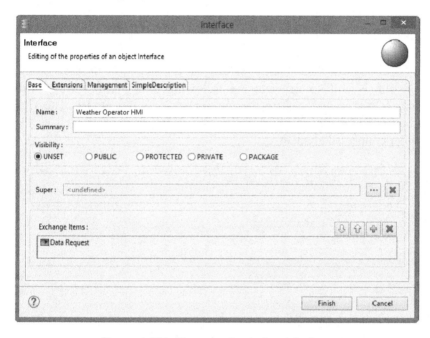

Figure 4.154. *Property sheet of an Interface*

We can do the same for the Actor "Earth Atmosphere", and Capella creates a second Interface "Environmental Conditions", which contains the EI "Air Particles". It is then possible to ask Capella to automatically create two new types of diagram:

– Contextual Component Detailed Interface (CDI);

– Contextual Component External Interface (CEI).

Figure 4.155. *Contextual Interface diagrams*

Although we have only created a few EIs in our case study, Capella is able to generate the following diagrams (Figures 1.156 and 1.157), which reflect the current state of the model. The CEI shows the Interfaces of a specific structural element as well as the other connected elements.

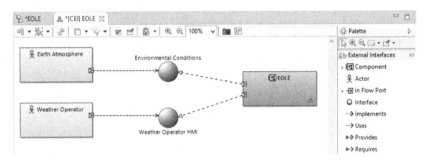

Figure 4.156. *CEI for EOLE. For a color version of the figure, see www.iste.co.uk/roques/arcadia.zip*

NOTE (Arcadia Rule).– An interaction role describes the operating instructions of an Interface for a Component by qualifying the allocation of the Interface to a Component Port of the Component. A role is therefore given to a Port and an Interface. In the largely majoritarian case of dependency from the data (matter, flow, messages, events, shared data, etc.), only two roles are defined: the role (implements/provides) of the provider and the role (uses/requires) of the consumer.

In our example, EOLE provides the Interfaces used by the Actors. This means that the System is able to receive the data created by the Actors and react to it.

NOTE.– EOLE receives the data and flows from the Actors, yet also provides the Interfaces. The notions of *provide/use* for interfaces come from object concepts, and particularly from UML. They are not very intuitive for a systems engineer without a computer science background. The graphical notation also comes directly from the UML component diagram [ROQ 04]: dashed arrow for dependency, and dashed line with a triangular arrowhead at the end for implementation.

The other Interface diagram is the CDI, which shows the details of provided or required Interfaces of a structural element, i.e. all of the EIs referenced.

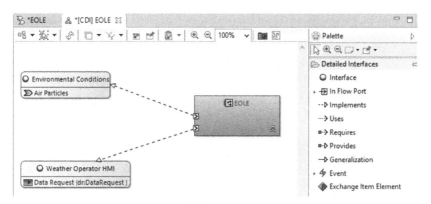

Figure 4.157. *CDI for EOLE. For a color version of the figure, see www.iste.co.uk/roques/arcadia.zip*

Complete Example of Modeling with Capella: Logical Architecture

5.1. Main concepts and diagrams

Capella integrates methodological guiding in the form of *Activity Explorer*. This lists the different activities and the different diagrams that can be made in terms of the engineering level concerned. In this case, this is namely Logical Architecture. Figure 5.1 first specifies the activities, and then we will detail the possible diagrams throughout the case study.

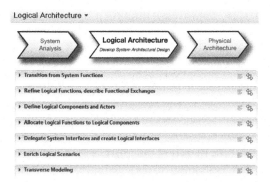

Figure 5.1. *Methodological activities in terms of Logical Architecture*

NOTE.– Be careful, let us recall that even if Arcadia is a method, the modeling process is totally flexible. The methodological activities presented in *Activity Explorer* are almost all optional and can be used in any order, as well as for diagrams.

We will therefore make an arbitrary but reasoned choice again here, for creating diagrams. We will start by automatically recovering the Functions and Actors issued from the System level to start our Logical level. Then, inside the System, we will create perennial Logical Components that are independent from any technological choice. At the same time, we will decide on allocating Logical level Functions to these components, and we may be led to break down the Functions issued from the System level or to complete them. We will then work on the Ports and the Component Exchanges issued from the System level that we will delegate to the Logical Components and we will add internal Component Exchanges, if necessary.

To keep in line with the book's aim, we will make modeling choices that enable the case study to maintain its simplicity. The model of the real project would certainly be more complex.

5.2. Moving from the System level to the Logical level

The previous System Analysis consisted of functionally analyzing the System seen as a "black box" to specify its expected behavior, as well as exhaustively identifying important external exchanges with the Actors.

Logical Architecture, on the other hand, starts to "open the box" to identify structural elements called Logical Components as well as their properties and relations. The important rule to comply with is to force ourselves to exclude all technological considerations or implementation choices. This will be the very objective of the Physical Architecture to define the "true" concrete components, which will constitute the System.

Excluding all technological considerations as a design choice will not however prevent us from beginning to take the Non-Functional Constraints into account. Operating Safety, Performance, etc., requirements can thus lead us to group the Functions together in different Components. In the same way, the Product Line Engineering (PLE) problem must begin to be considered from this level onwards to separate the "generic" and reusable Logical Components of the Logical Components specific to the current project. Finally, good important practice can be outlined as follows: Logical Architecture must be stable throughout the whole duration of the project. This will probably not be the case for Physical Architecture, especially if the System must have a long life-span, due to the technological novelties that will occur and the new Physical Components that may cause large parts of the architecture to be called into question.

To start the Logical level from the work performed on the System level, Capella proposes transitions like those that we used when we went from the Operational Analysis to the System Analysis. We can thus create as many Logical Functions as System Functions, while also keeping the Functional Exchanges and the Functional Chains. We apply this first transition based on the *Activity Explorer*.

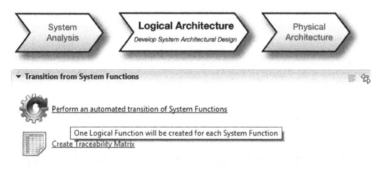

Figure 5.2. *Transition tool for the Functions to the Logical level*

We are now looking at a simple transition case, and pressing on the "*Apply*" button will allow us to recover everything in one go. The result is visible in the *Project Explorer* where model elements now exist in the *Logical Functions* folder.

Let us recall that Capella automatically creates a Realization Link between each Logical element (Function, Functional Exchange, Functional Chain) and the Source System element. We also recall that the transitions are iterative and incremental and that if we notice that a

System Function is missing when working on the Logical level, we must absolutely add it to the System level and apply the transition again.

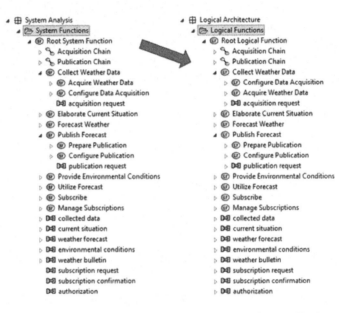

Figure 5.3. *Result of the Functional Transition in Project Explorer*

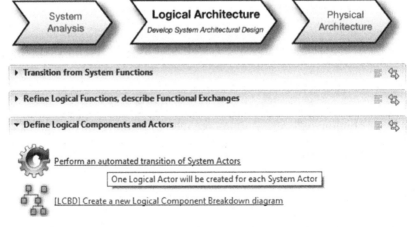

Figure 5.4. *Transition tool for the Actors to the Logical level*

We now apply the transition of the external Actors. In most cases, the Actors identified on the System level will be exactly the same as on the Logical and Physical levels. The automatic transition (iterative and incremental) is thus particularly useful for this type of model element.

We are here looking at a simple transition case, and pressing on the *Apply* button will allow us to recover everything in one go. The result is visible in the *Project Explorer* where the model elements now exist in the *Logical Actors* folder. Capella also automatically recovers the Component Ports and the Component Exchanges between the System and the Actors, which will ease the Logical Architecture work enormously later. It also keeps the Allocations of Functional Exchanges to Component Exchanges.

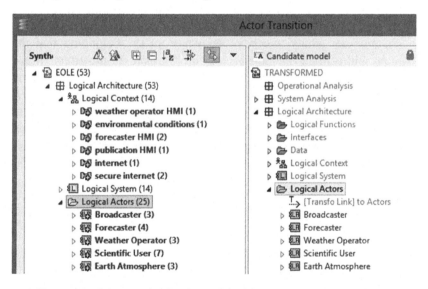

Figure 5.5. *Dialogue for the Actor Transition tool to the Logical level*

In the *Project Explorer*, we will check that we have properly recovered the Actors and the Component Exchanges. The Ports are not visible in the *Project Explorer* by default, but nevertheless they are in the *Semantic Browser*, as well as the Allocation and Realization relations.

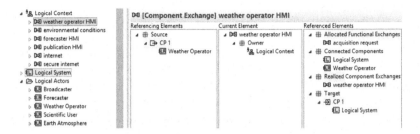

Figure 5.6. *Verification of the Actor transition result*

5.3. Logical Components

As indicated above, the Logical Architecture starts by identifying structural elements called Logical Components by forcing ourselves to exclude all technological consideration or implementation choice.

In our case study, we have known from the beginning that the System will contain two Subsystems: an acquisition Subsystem "in the air" and a processing Subsystem on the ground. We are not yet talking about a helium balloon, which is an implementation choice that is part of the Physical Architecture world. By the way, it is good practice to name the Logical Components and Physical Components differently, and only attributing the names containing references to a precise technology to the Physical Components.

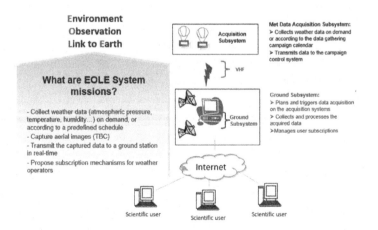

Figure 5.7. *Reminder of the EOLE System's design brief*

NOTE (Arcadia Rule).– Be careful. The notion of Subsystem does not exist in Arcadia. In System Analysis, we can only have a single model element called System. If we want to model Subsystems, we need to be on an internal, Logical or Physical, Architecture Level. If we want to be able to then consider each Subsystem as a full member System, with its own System Analysis, Logical then Physical Architecture, we must model each Subsystem in a specific Capella model. The ideal being to maintain coherency between the external Exchanges of the different Subsystems in the "global" model of the encompassing System. This is exactly what allows us to do the System to Subsystem Transition add-on, which can be downloaded from the Website www.polarsys.org/capella/download.html. We will illustrate these very interesting capabilities further in this chapter on Logical Architecture.

So, we are going to create two Logical Components corresponding to the two Subsystems. To do this, we can use a Breakdown diagram (*LCBD*) or directly use an Architecture diagram (*LAB*). We could even start from an Exchange Scenario (*LES*) and by creating vertical lines representing new Components, as explained in the System level.

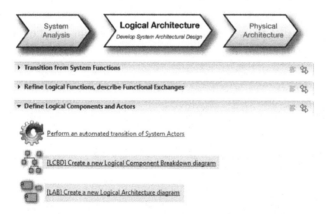

Figure 5.8. *Diagrams for creating Logical Components*

The most efficient way here is to start directly from the Architecture Diagram, especially as the Breakdown diagram can be performed automatically by Capella, *a posteriori*. Like in the case of the Architecture diagram on the System level (System Architecture Blank (SAB)), the *LAB* will not be empty either. As a matter of fact, Capella automatically inserts a box representing the System on the Logical level (*Logical System*) that enables the Component Ports and the Component Exchanges issued from the Actor Transition to materialize. The Logical System thus constitutes a very practical "reminder" that prevents us from forgetting to delegate the external Ports to the Components. Once more, Capella makes the modeler's life easy because of its thorough knowledge of the Arcadia approach.

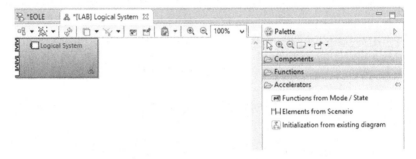

Figure 5.9. *Beginning of the Logical Architecture Blank diagram (LAB)*

We are going to create two Logical Components inside the *Logical System* by expanding and centering the same.

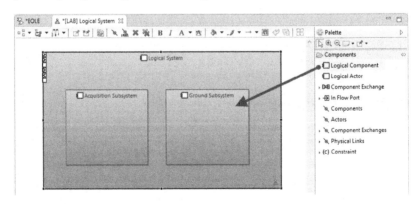

Figure 5.10. *Creating Logical Components in LAB*

NOTE.– In the case of the EOLE System, the box representing the *Logical System* will no longer exist in Logical and Physical Architecture. In the end, the only concrete structural containers will be the balloon and the ground station. Thus, we can change the color of the *Logical System* to indicate that it is not really a Component and must no longer have Ports by the time our work is finished. Be careful: if the System on the Physical level still had a concrete external envelope, this would not be the same, and the external Ports would need to be conserved until the end.

Before moving onto allocating the Functions, we insert the Actors already in the diagram. We note that the *Component Exchanges* issued from the Transition automatically appear in the diagram.

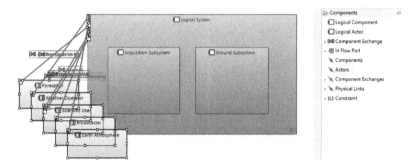

Figure 5.11. *Inserting the Logical Actors in the LAB*

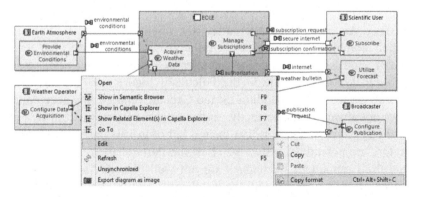

Figure 5.12. *Copy of the format of an SAB. For a color version of the figure, see www.iste.co.uk/roques/arcadia.zip*

The graphic positioning of the Actors is far from optimal, and unfortunately even still with the *Arrange All* command in the diagram. In contrast, there is an efficient way to remedy this by copying and pasting the layout of a diagram like the System level. To do this, we will go back to the complete *SAB* and call upon the context-sensitive *Edit–Copy format* command, as in Figure 5.12.

We are now going to paste the format in the *LAB*. After having spread the Actors and changed the color of the *Logical System* as indicated, we obtain the following diagram (Figure 5.13).

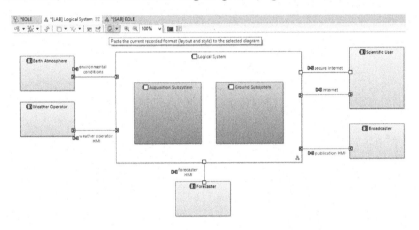

Figure 5.13. *LAB continued. For a color version of the figure, see www.iste.co.uk/roques/arcadia.zip*

NOTE.– An interesting alternative for obtaining an *LAB* diagram, which graphically resembles a similar diagram of the System level (*SAB*), consists of using the accelerator called *Initialization from existing diagram*, visible in the Palette of Figure 5.9. We have not proceeded thus as, depending on the Capella version, this accelerator does not always work perfectly. In the current version (1.1.1), the box of the *Logical System* is still at the top left of the diagram, whereas the Actors are positioned properly. Thus, the Ports of the *Logical System* and the Component Exchanges are not well placed. As soon as this minor problem is corrected, the accelerator will be the most efficient means of creating an *LAB* based on an *SAB*.

5.4. Allocation of the Logical Functions

We have indicated that the Transition from the Actors conserved their Function Allocations. We can therefore very easily insert them into the *LAB* diagram using the same System level Palette command: *Insert All Allocated Functions*. We could also have inserted the Functions before applying the format copy–paste to save time, but we can still do it again by selecting the Actors in the *SAB* before copying the format.

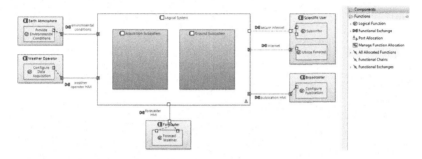

Figure 5.14. *Inserting the Functions allocated to the Actors in the LAB. For a color version of the figure, see www.iste.co.uk/roques/arcadia.zip*

NOTE.– We note that the Functions that were allocated to EOLE in the System level are currently not allocated. Capella knows that we have transitioned them either to allocate them to one of the Logical Components, or to break them down and allocate their subfunctions. It is therefore necessary that they are not yet allocated so as to be able to make one choice or another. It therefore would have hardly been wise to allocate them automatically to the *Logical System* ….

We will now proceed to Allocate each Function of the System to one of the Logical Components. Our example will voluntarily remain very simple, even simplistic, for educational purposes. For example, we could have started to break down the "Acquire Data" Function according to the types of different data (temperature, pressure, etc.), but we will only do it on the Physical level. Similarly, we should have started to process the communication needs between the ground and the airborne, as the Weather Operator will probably not be able to communicate directly with the Acquisition Subsystem, but instead through the Ground Subsystem.

Thus, we simply allocate the "Acquire Meteorological Data" Function to the Acquisition Component, and the three other Functions to the Ground Component. To do this, we will use the *Manage Function Allocation* command of the *LAB* Palette. Note that the Functional Exchanges are automatically displayed as soon as their target and source Functions are shown in the diagram. The transition from the System level has also conserved the allocations from the Functional Exchanges to the Component Exchanges.

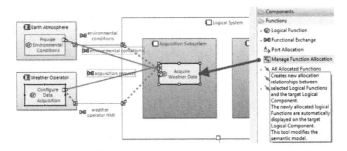

Figure 5.15. *Beginning of the Function allocation to the Logical Components. For a color version of the figure, see www.iste.co.uk/roques/arcadia.zip*

We complete the Allocation before graphically improving the diagram. By moving the Ports and optimizing the placing of the Functions, we quickly end up with the following diagram (Figure 5.16).

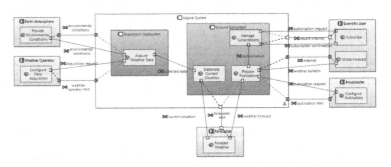

Figure 5.16. *End of Functions Allocation to the Logical Components. For a color version of the figure, see www.iste.co.uk/roques/arcadia.zip*

Like in the upper level, we can easily verify that we have allocated all the Functions. To do this, you just need to try to apply the *Manage Function Allocation* command to any structural element again: if the selection choice is empty, this means that all the Functions have been allocated. Of course, the *Model Validation* can also be used.

We previously indicated that in our case, the *Logical System* does not really exist and above all, allows the Component Ports and the Component Exchanges issued from the Transition from the Actors to materialize. Thus, it constitutes a very practical "reminder'" that prevents us from forgetting to delegate the external Ports to the Components, which we will now do. To do this, we just need to drag-drop the Component Ports from the border of the *Logical System* toward the Logical Component concerned.

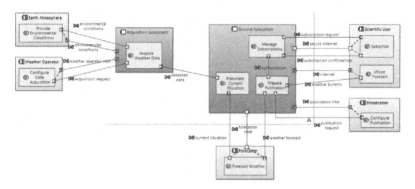

Figure 5.17. *Dropping the external Ports on the Logical Components. For a color version of the figure, see www.iste.co.uk/roques/arcadia.zip*

We verify that the *Logical System* no longer has any Ports. To do this, we will also change the color of its contour so that it almost no longer appears. We will also complete the Allocations of the Functional Ports, which were lost by dragging the Component Ports. To do this, we just need to open the Property Sheet of a Component Port and to select the Function Ports concerned in the *Allocated Ports* field.

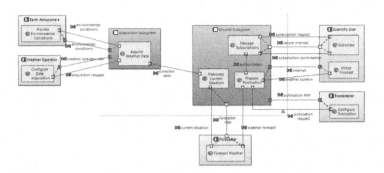

Figure 5.18. *Finalizing the dropping of the external Ports. For a color version of the figure, see www.iste.co.uk/roques/arcadia.zip*

On this level, we see that the Functional Exchange "collected data" crosses the borders of the two Components. It is therefore necessary to create a new internal Component Exchange to allocate it.

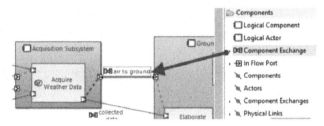

Figure 5.19. *Creating an internal Component Exchange. For a color version of the figure, see www.iste.co.uk/roques/arcadia.zip*

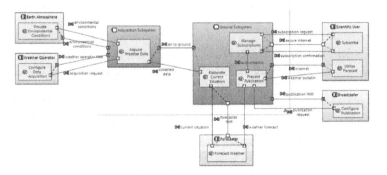

Figure 5.20. *Finalized LAB. For a color version of the figure, see www.iste.co.uk/roques/arcadia.zip*

The finalized diagram (Figure 5.20) becomes relatively complex, and it could be useful to clone it, and then from this, we derive two partial diagrams, each centered on a Subsystem.

5.5. System to Subsystem Transition

However, beyond the graphic simplification, we may want to delegate the modeling of each Subsystem to a different team, perhaps even to subcontracting companies. In this case, it would be very desirable to consider each Subsystem as a System in turn, with its own Capella model starting at the *SA* level. The Arcadia approach can effectively be applied recursively up to the level of the detail desired: System of Systems (SoS), complex System, Subsystem, equipment.

The ideal being to maintain coherence between the external exchanges of the different Subsystems in the "global" model of the encompassing System that we have just performed. This is exactly what allows us to do the System to Subsystem Transition add-on, which can be downloaded from the Capella Website.

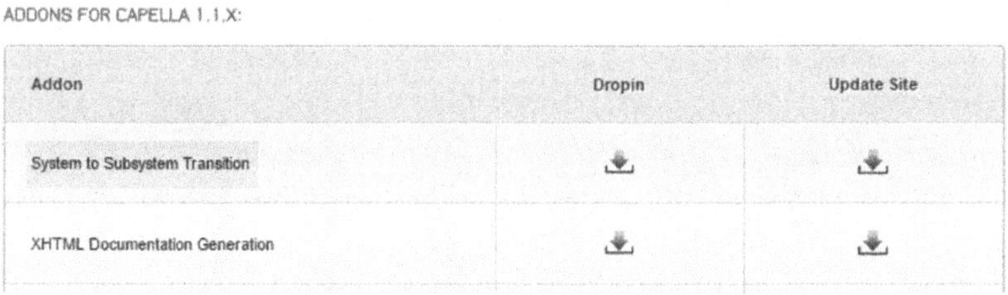

ADDONS FOR CAPELLA 1.1.X:

Addon	Dropin	Update Site
System to Subsystem Transition	⬇	⬇
XHTML Documentation Generation	⬇	⬇

Figure 5.21. *Downloading space for Capella add-ons*

If we select a Logical Component (or a Physical Component), it is possible to ask the tool to start a new Capella Model of the selected Component. The Component in question becomes the *System* model element of the *SA* level of the new model; the Actors and Components to which it was connected become the Actors of the System level in the new model. The Functions, Functional Chains, Types, Exchange Items (EI), Scenarios, etc., are also propagated toward the models of the Subsystems.

The modeler in charge of each Subsystem must consider the SA Level of its Component as imposed by the global System level, but it is completely free to perform the Logical Architecture and the Physical Architecture of the Subsystem in turn. This transition is also iterative and incremental, which enables the modifications of interfaces between the Subsystems to be managed efficiently by applying again the transition of the System level toward the Subsystems.

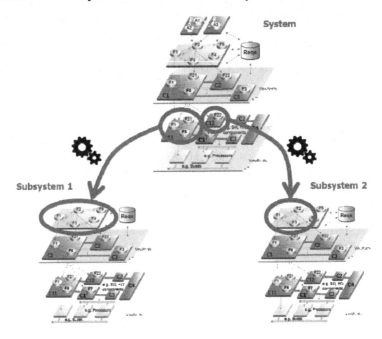

Figure 5.22. *Principle of the System to Subsystem add-on. For a color version of the figure, see www.iste.co.uk/roques/arcadia.zip*

We illustrate the use of this add-on on our case study. We imagine that we want to design and develop the two Acquisition and Ground Subsystems by different teams, or even to subcontract them completely. It is therefore possible to stop the global "System" model on the current detail level, and to perform two transitions, one for each Subsystem.

We are going to perform the transition for the Acquisition Subsystem. After having installed the add-on as indicated in the illustration procedure, we have an additional command at our disposal in the *Project Explorer* by right clicking on a Logical (or Physical) Component: *System to Subsystem Transition*. There are even two possibilities, the horizontal transition being just an extraction of a component toward a new model but staying within the same Arcadia level. We are going to perform the so-called vertical transition.

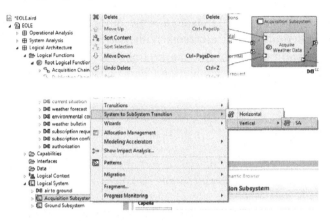

Figure 5.23. *Context-sensitive call of the System to Subsystem Transition command*

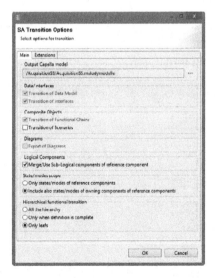

Figure 5.24. *System to Subsystem Transition command options*

Capella then opens a window (Figure 5.24) that enables the transition to be guided. In particular, we are going to specify whether a new project needs to be created or if an existing project is to be used. For example, we will create a new project called "Acquisition SS", with only the mandatory Arcadia levels *SA*, *LA* and *PA*.

Capella then opens a *diff/merge* type window, like for the transitions between levels inside a same model, to allow the modeler to ignore certain model elements if they wish. We can see that the Functions and Functional Exchanges linked to the acquisition are well proposed, as well as the acquisition Chain.

Figure 5.25. *Previsualization window of the transition*

In the same way, the Exchange Items and Types used in these Functional Exchanges are exported, as well as the two Actors bound to the Acquisition Subsystem. The other Subsystem (Ground) becomes an Actor in turn.

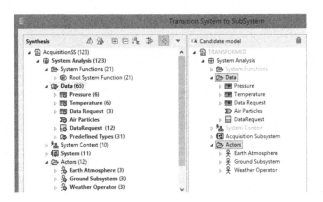

Figure 5.26. *Previsualization window of the transition continued*

The result is the creation of a new Capella model, visible in the *Project Explorer* and its *Activity Explorer*.

NOTE (Arcadia Rule).– By default, the *Activity Explorer* contains all the Arcadia levels, even if we have chosen to remove the optional levels when creating the project. To hide *OA* and *EPBS* in our example, we just need to modify the project preferences with the command *Window – Preferences – Activity Explorer – Management* and untick the unwanted levels. It is even possible to hide certain specific fields for the remaining levels.

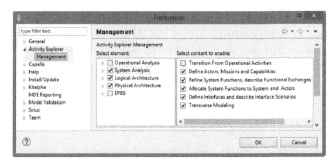

Figure 5.27. *Configuring the Activity Explorer display*

The result of hiding it is immediately visible.

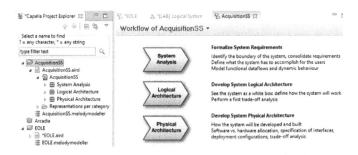

Figure 5.28. *Result of the Activity Explorer configuration*

We now open this new "Acquisition SS" model to verify that it contains the model elements wanted, and to quickly create some useful diagrams. The SAB diagram will be particularly relevant: we will see the Acquisition Subsystem with its Functions, surrounded by Actors and their Functions, with the Functional Exchanges and the Component Exchanges. When creating the *SAB*, the Acquisition Subsystem automatically appears with its Component Ports.

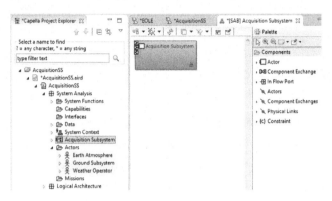

Figure 5.29. *Beginning of the SAB of the Acquisition SS*

We are going to insert the Actors (*Insert/Remove Actors*), then all the Functions at once (*Insert All Allocated Functions*). The Functional Exchanges and the Component Exchanges appear automatically.

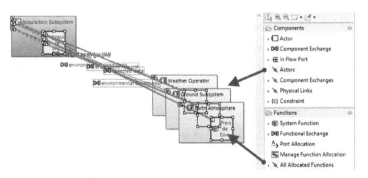

Figure 5.30. *Inserting the Actors and the Functions in the SAB*

Once the formatting is improved, we can definitely see that the *SAB* resembles a subset of the encompassing model's *LAB*, with the difference being that the second Subsystem became an Actor for the first.

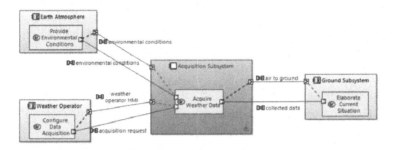

Figure 5.31. *Finalizing the SAB of the Subsystem. For a color version of the figure, see www.iste.co.uk/roques/arcadia.zip*

We can even add the Acquisition Functional Chain that was automatically transitioned with the Subsystem.

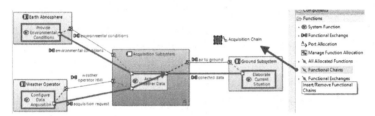

Figure 5.32. *Display of the Functional Chain in the SAB. For a color version of the figure, see www.iste.co.uk/roques/arcadia.zip*

The *EI* associated with the Functional Exchanges have been conserved, as can be verified by applying the adequate filter.

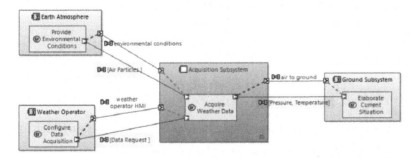

Figure 5.33. *Display of the EI on the FE in the SAB. For a color version of the figure, see www.iste.co.uk/roques/arcadia.zip*

This transition toward a new model has been performed for educational purposes, to give a concrete illustration of the add-on use. In the rest of the book, we will continue with the EOLE model in a unique model until the *EPBS*.

5.6. Scenarios on the Logical level

In this section, we only use Exchange Scenarios mainly to show Capella's capabilities to set up a Scenario based on another from the upper level. We have illustrated the three types of Scenario (Functional, Exchange, Interface) in sections 4.7 and 4.9.

NOTE (Arcadia rule).– A Logical (or Physical) Scenario describes the Logical (or Physical) Components within the framework of a particular System Capability. On these two levels, we therefore also find a *Capabilities* folder for structuring the Scenarios. However, we note that these are not new Capabilities, but rather the realization of System level Capabilities. Moreover, if we bother to look more closely, the folder is actually called *Capability Realization Pkg* and the Capabilities contained are called *Capability Realizations.*

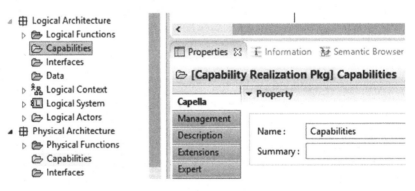

Figure 5.34. *Capabilities folder on the LA and PA levels*

Let us start again from the System level acquisition Exchange Scenario (SES).

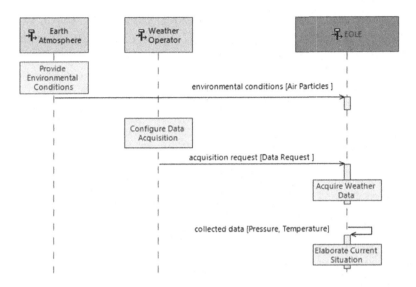

Figure 5.35. *Reminder of the System level acquisition Exchange Scenario*

The Logical Actors will be the same as the System level; however, the EOLE vertical line will be replaced by the necessary and sufficient subset of Logical Components following the Logical Functions allocation. In this example, we need two Components because the "Acquire Weather Data" Function is performed by the Acquisition Subsystem and the "Elaborate Current Situation" Function is performed by the Ground Subsystem. On the other hand, in the broadcast SES (Figure 4.89), the "Ground" Subsystem would be sufficient.

Capella knows the System level Scenario. It knows how to travel through the realization links between the Logical Functions and the System Functions and it knows the allocation of the Logical Functions to the Logical Components. The tool is thus capable of proposing an automatic initialization of a Logical level Scenario based on a System level Scenario. This will obviously also be the case between Logical and Physical levels.

So, we ask the tool to perform this initialization by positioning ourselves either in the previous diagram or in the Scenario in *Project*

Explorer, and by activating the contextual command: *Transitions – System Exchange Scenario to Logical Exchange Scenario Initialization*.

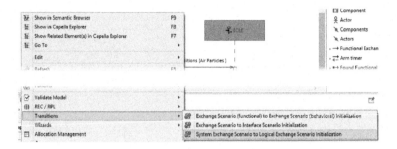

Figure 5.36. *Transition from the System level Exchange Scenario*

After the transition, Capella first created a Capability Realization with the same name as the System Capability, and an Exchange Scenario also with the same name as the SES. The vertical lines of the Logical Scenario represent the same Actors plus the two Logical Components as anticipated.

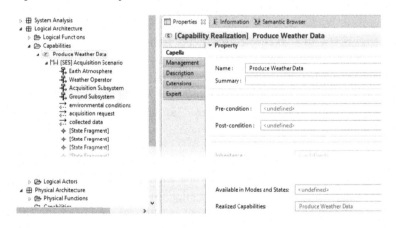

Figure 5.37. *Result of the transition from the System Scenario in Explorer*

Now all we need to do is rename the Scenario in *LES* and create the diagram using the contextual command: *New Diagram/Table... – Exchange Scenario.*

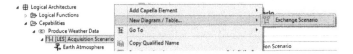

Figure 5.38. *Creating the Logical Scenario diagram*

The Scenario diagram thus created is automatically displayed as in Figure 5.39. We note that the "collected data" message, which is reflexive at the System level, now goes from the Acquisition Subsystem to the Ground Subsystem.

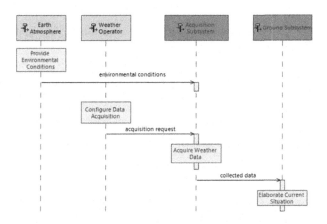

Figure 5.39. *Automatically initialized Logical Scenario diagram. For a color version of the figure, see www.iste.co.uk/roques/arcadia.zip*

We note that the Function displays have been kept, and positioned on the right Component. We also note that the EI associated with the messages have also been preserved. It is thus possible to show the EI on the FE by applying the same filter as the System level.

It would be entirely possible to now add Constraints or even new Messages or new Functions corresponding to the created model elements based on the Logical level. Therefore, the command is called "initialization": it ensures that the exchanges are coherent with the Actors, but allows enrichment on the level concerned. We are going to create a Duration Constraint, as we did to the System level on the Functional Scenario, but this time on the execution of the Acquisition Function.

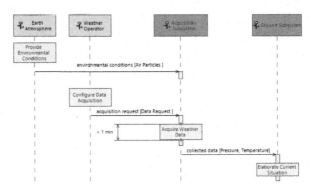

Figure 5.40. *Completed Logical Scenario diagram. For a color version of the figure, see www.iste.co.uk/roques/arcadia.zip*

To complete the illustration of the System to Subsystem transition possibilities, we try to apply this transition again by ticking the *Transition of Scenarios* option. This time, a Capability and a Scenario are created in the target model of the Subsystem.

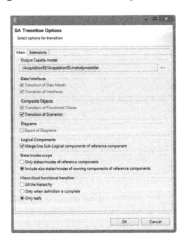

Figure 5.41. *Additional option of the System to Subsystem transition. For a color version of the figure, see www.iste.co.uk/roques/arcadia.zip*

The incremental transition opens a *diff/merge* type window.

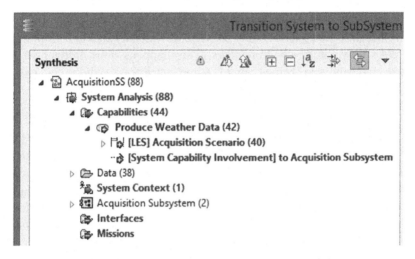

Figure 5.42. *Incremental application of the Subsystem transition*

Now we just need to rename the Scenario and ask Capella to create the corresponding diagram.

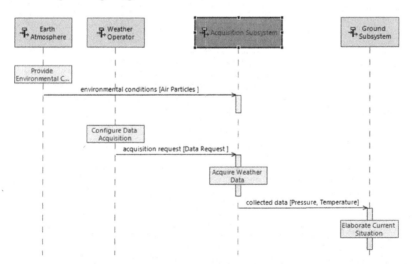

Figure 5.43. *Subsystem Scenario generated by transition. For a color version of the figure, see www.iste.co.uk/roques/arcadia.zip*

5.7. Logical subcomponents

To complete this small and fast synopsis of the Logical Architecture level, let us study the case in which a Logical Component breaks down into subcomponents. This happens quite frequently on real projects and brings about some intricacies when delegating Component Ports, which we will illustrate in our EOLE example.

We are going to start from the Architecture diagram and simplify it by only keeping the Actors and Components, which are connected to the Ground Subsystem. Then, we are going to create two logical subcomponents inside the Ground Subsystem: a data-processing Component and a web publication Component. With a simple drag – drop, we are going to allocate the "Elaborate Current Situation" Function to the data-processing Component, and the "Prepare Publication" and "Manage Subscriptions" Functions to the web publication Component. The result of this preliminary work is given in Figure 5.44.

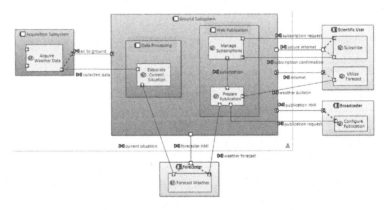

Figure 5.44. *Structural breakdown of the Ground Subsystem. For a color version of the figure, see www.iste.co.uk/roques/arcadia.zip*

NOTE (Arcadia rule).– The Functions breakdown and the Components breakdown are not governed by the same Arcadia rules. We have already seen that the broken down Functions should no longer have input/output Ports: only the leaf (or terminal) Functions can have Function Ports and can be allocated. This is not the same for the

Components. The Logical (or Physical) Components that are broken down can, nevertheless, still possess Component Ports as such, which it will need for connecting the Ports of their subcomponents. It is quite easy to understand the use of this rule for Physical Components. It is applied in the same way in Logical Architecture. However, this is not obligatory, and certain Components may not have external Ports: this is a modeling choice.

Therefore, there are two types of modeling possible for our Ground Subsystem:

– either by considering that it is only a pure container, like the Logical System in our example, and that only the subcomponents possess Component Ports;

– or by considering that the Subsystem keeps its own Ports, which will allow it to apply a System/Subsystem transition when required, but the subcomponents also have their Component Ports, connected to the first.

We are going to illustrate the two alternative solutions in the following. If we first assume that the Ground Subsystem is only a pure container, we will just need to drag–drop each of its ports toward the adequate subcomponent. A difficulty will occur in terms of the two-way Port connected to the Forecaster, and we will see the solution in the following. We have changed the color of the Ground Subsystem to white so as to visually reinforce the subcomponents.

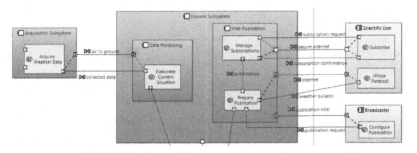

Figure 5.45. *First solution: Ground Subsystem as a pure container. For a color version of the figure, see www.iste.co.uk/roques/arcadia.zip*

The second solution is a bit more complex and calls upon a new concept: Delegation. As a matter of fact, we are going to leave the Component Ports on the Ground Subsystem, and "delegate" them to the subcomponents. To do this, Capella proposes a specific command in the palette, under *Component Exchange*, called *Delegation*. This command, activated from a Port of the container Component, creates a new Port in the same direction on the contained Component and connects it to the first one by a Component Exchange of kind Delegation.

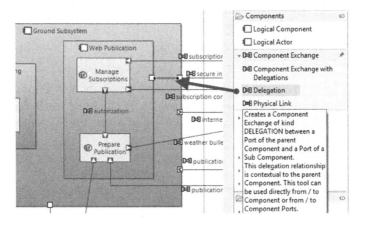

Figure 5.46. *Delegation connector*

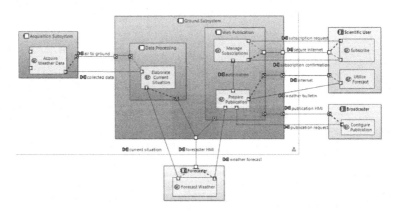

Figure 5.47. *Second solution: Port Delegation. For a color version of the figure, see www.iste.co.uk/roques/arcadia.zip*

If we repeat this work on all the Ports of the Subsystem and finalize all the Functional Port allocations, we end up with Figure 5.47.

NOTE.– A "classic" *Component Exchange* connects two Ports of opposite directions. A *Delegation-type Component Exchange* connects two Ports of the same direction. Capella knows this and creates Ports in the right direction every time.

6

Complete Example of Modeling with Capella: Physical Architecture

6.1. Main concepts and diagrams

Capella integrates a methodological guide in the form of the *Activity Explorer*. This lists the different activities and the different diagrams that can be created on the relevant engineering level, namely here Physical Architecture. Figure 6.1 specifies the activities first, and then we will detail the diagrams possible as the case study unwinds.

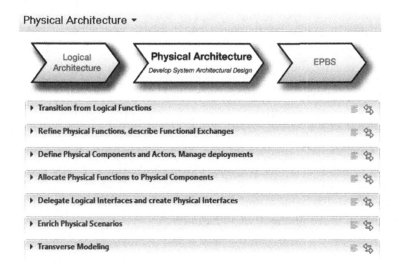

Figure 6.1. *Methodological activities from the "Physical Architecture" level*

NOTE.– Warning: we recall that even if Arcadia is a method, the modeling process is totally flexible. The methodological activities presented in the *Activity Explorer* are almost all optional and may be created in any order whatsoever, just as for diagrams.

So, again here, we are going to make an arbitrary but reasoned choice for creating the diagrams. We will start by automatically recovering the Functions and the Actors issued from the Logical level to start our Physical level. We will then create concrete Physical Components inside the system by making the technological choices this time. At the same time, we will decide to allocate the Physical level Functions to these components, and we may be led to break down the Functions issued from the Logical level or to complete them.

In keeping with the book's goal, we will make some modeling choices that allow the case study to retain its simplicity. The model of the real project would obviously be more complex.

6.2. Moving from the Logical level to the Physical level

The previous Logical Architecture started by "opening the black box" in order to identify the structural elements called Logical Components, as well as their properties and relations. The important rule that we have followed is to ensure that you exclude all technological considerations or implementation choices on this level. This is exactly the objective of the Physical Architecture in defining the "real" concrete components that comprise the system.

To start the Physical level based on the Logical level, Capella proposes transitions similar to those that we used when we went from the Operational Analysis to the System Analysis, then from the System Analysis to the Logical Architecture. Thus, we can create as many Physical Functions as Logical Functions, by also keeping the Functional Exchanges and Functional Chains. We apply this first transition based on the *Activity Explorer*.

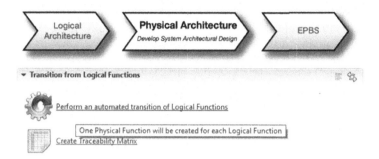

Figure 6.2. *Functional Transition tool toward the Physical level*

Here again, we are looking at a simple transition case, and pressing on the *Apply* button will enable us to recover everything in one go. The result is visible in the *Project Explorer* in which some model elements now exist in the *Physical Functions* folder.

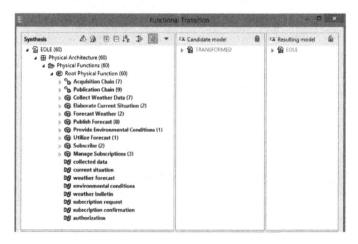

Figure 6.3. *Functional Transition dialogue window*

We recall that Capella automatically creates a realization link between each Physical element (Function, Functional Exchange, Functional Chain) and the corresponding Logical element. We also recall that the transitions are iterative and incremental and if in working on the Physical level, we notice that a Logical Function is missing, perhaps a System Function, it is absolutely essential to roll back to the highest level so as to add it and then apply the transition again.

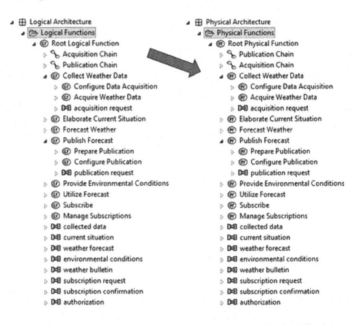

Figure 6.4. *Result of the Functional Transition in Project Explorer*

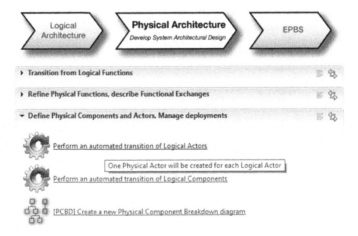

Figure 6.5. *Transition tool from the Actors toward the Physical level*

We now apply the transition of the external Actors (Figure 6.5). In most cases, the Actors identified on the Logical level will be exactly the same on the Physical level. The automatic transition (iterative and incremental) is therefore once again particularly useful for this type of model element.

Here, we are looking again at a simple transition case, and pressing on the *Apply* button could enable us to recover everything in one go. But to simplify the model for educational purposes, we will restrict the transition.

As a matter of fact, Capella also proposes to recover the Component Ports and the Component Exchanges between the System, which here means the Logical Components, and the Actors. In fact, it also proposes to recover the Logical Components, and to transform them into Behavior Physical Components. Yet, we prefer to completely master creating the Behavior Components on the Physical level: the granularity level will be finer than in the Logical level, the names refer to the technological choices, etc. Therefore, we are going to prevent the transition from the Logical Components and the Component Exchanges with the Actors.

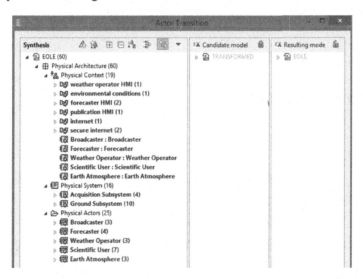

Figure 6.6. *Dialogue for the transition of Actors toward the Logical level*

NOTE.– It is possible to finely master the automatic descending transitions proposed by Capella. Once we master the transitional *diff/merge* type interface, it is easy to limit the transition to a subset of elements, knowing that we will always be able to complete it later.

We are simply going to choose to ignore the transition from the Logical Components by right clicking on *Ignore* on the container of the proposed Behavior Components: *Physical System*.

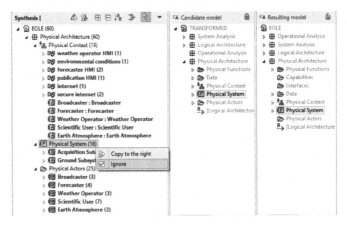

Figure 6.7. *Action on the transition of Components toward the Physical level*

The *Ignore* action will modify the *Resulting model* with respect to the *Candidate model*, and will prevent the transition from the Behavior Components, as desired.

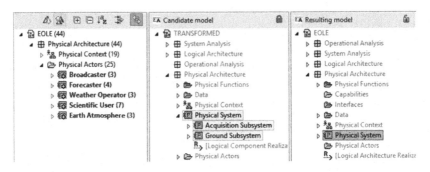

Figure 6.8. *Following the action for the non-transition of Components*

The result of the transition is then visible in *Project Explorer* where the model elements now exist in the folder *Physical Actors*, to which the Physical Functions are allocated, to the image of the Logical and System levels.

Figure 6.9. *Verification of the Actors' transition result*

6.3. Physical Components

In our case study, from the beginning, we know that the system will contain two subsystems: an Acquisition Subsystem "in the air" for which the state of the art consists of using a sounding balloon inflated with helium and a Ground Processing Subsystem. On the Logical level, we have not yet spoken about technological choices, which is now contrary to the objective of Physical Architecture. We recall that it is good practice to name the Logical and Physical Components differently, and to attribute names containing references to a technology specific only to Physical Components.

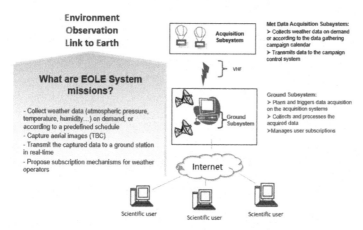

Figure 6.10. *Recall of the "EOLE" system design brief*

NOTE (Arcadia rule).– There are two types of Physical Components in Arcadia. A Behavior Physical Component is a component of the System, responsible for performing some of the Functions assigned to the system, by interacting with other Behavior Components and with that of the external Actors. A Node Physical Component is a component that hosts a certain number of Behavior Components, by providing them with the resources required for them to operate and interact with their environment. A Behavior Component is hosted by one single Node Physical Component.

We are therefore going to first create two Node Physical Components corresponding to the two subsystems as well as subcomponents of the same type, for example a probe holder in the sounding balloon, and two computer servers in the ground station. To do this, we can use a Physical Component Breakdown diagram (*PCBD*) or a Physical Architecture Blank (*PAB*) diagram directly.

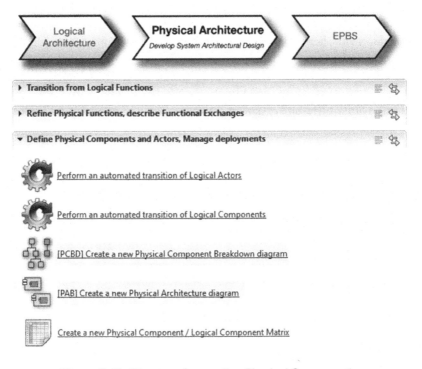

Figure 6.11. *Diagrams for creating Physical Components*

The most efficient method here is to start directly with the Architecture diagram, especially as the Breakdown diagram may be realized automatically by Capella later. Unlike the upper levels, the *PAB* will be empty at first.

The palette on the right is the most complex of all the diagrams proposed by Capella. As a matter of fact, in this type of diagram, we are going to be able to manipulate three types of concepts:

– Node Physical Components (yellow rectangles), which may contain other Node Components;

– Behavior Physical Components (blue rectangles), which will be deployed on the Node Physical Components;

– Physical Functions (green rectangles), which will be allocated to the Behavior Physical Components.

And we often find additional accelerators in the last group of commands.

Figure 6.12. *PAB (Physical Architecture Blank) Palette. For a color version of the figure, see www.iste.co.uk/roques/arcadia.zip*

So, let us start by creating the Node Physical Components in order to then deploy Behavior Physical Components to which the system's Functions will be allocated. A first draft is shown by Figure 6.13.

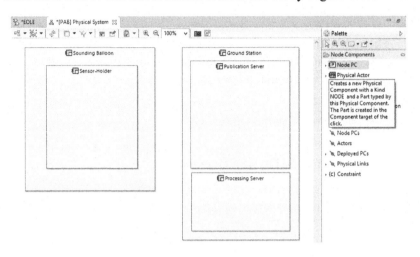

Figure 6.13. *First draft of the PAB with the Node Components. For a color version of the figure, see www.iste.co.uk/roques/arcadia.zip*

If we open the Property Sheet of a Physical Component, we note that the "Behavior/Node" nature is a postcreation modifiable property, and that there is also a *Physical Component Kind* property that allows the component type to be specified: software, hardware, computer, etc. For example, here, the two servers of the ground station will be marked as *Hardware Computer*.

NOTE.– It is possible to model a *Person* type Physical Component. This is particularly useful for a system whose operators are stakeholders, from the client's viewpoint. In this case, as the system operators are inside it, they must not be modeled as Actors of the System level, but rather as internal Components, on the Logical and Physical levels. Warning: the man–machine interfaces of the operators will not be visible on the System Analysis level, unlike those of the end users.

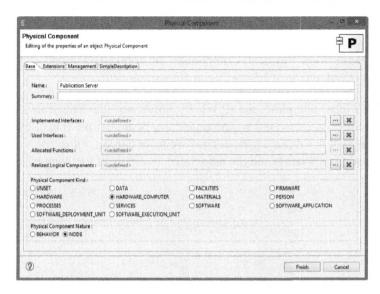

Figure 6.14. *Property Sheet of a Physical Component*

We continue by creating and deploying Behavior Components on the Node Components because of the *Deploy Behavior PC* command of the PAB palette. For example, we are going to deploy two different sensors on the sensor holder, as well as the software applications in the servers of the ground station.

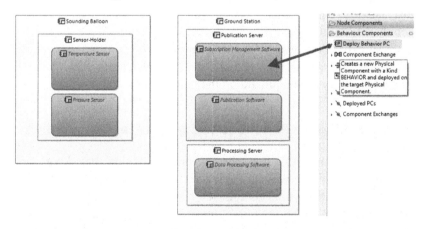

Figure 6.15. *Deployment of Behavior Components. For a color version of the figure, see www.iste.co.uk/roques/arcadia.zip*

NOTE (Arcadia rule).– We recall the rules associated with the deployment relation. A Behavior Component is hosted by one and only one Node Physical Component. In contrast, a Node Physical Component may host several Behavior Components.

We can complete the PAB by inserting the Physical Actors automatically recovered by the transition. Note that the transition also propagated the Actor Ports, even if we have chosen not to recover the Logical Components and the associated Component Exchanges.

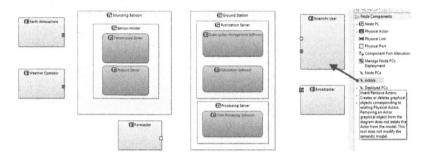

Figure 6.16. *Inserting the Physical Actors in the PAB. For a color version of the figure, see www.iste.co.uk/roques/arcadia.zip*

All we have to do now is to add the Functions. Those of the Actors have been recovered automatically by the descending transition: we just need to insert them graphically (*Insert Allocated Functions* command on the palette). Those of the System have also been automatically recovered by the descending transition but will need to be allocated to one single Behavior Physical Component (*Manage Function Allocation* command on the palette).

6.4. Allocating the Functions to the Physical Components

We have indicated that the Actors' transition has kept their Function allocations. We can therefore easily insert them into the *PAB* diagram using the same command of the palette as on the Logical level: *Insert All Allocated Functions*. However, beware: unlike the upper levels where the command worked on the background of the diagram, this time they need to be applied to each Actor. Then, we can copy–paste the format from the *LAB* onwards to position the Functions and their Ports automatically.

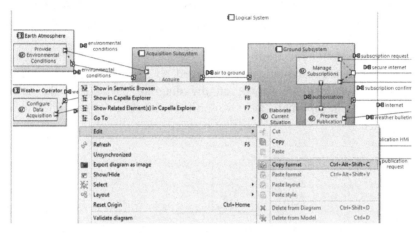

Figure 6.17. *Copying the LAB format*

We then obtain the following diagram. Note that we could even have avoided manually repositioning the Actors, by taking advantage of the *format copy–paste* from the *LAB* after having inserted the Actors in bulk then their Functions.

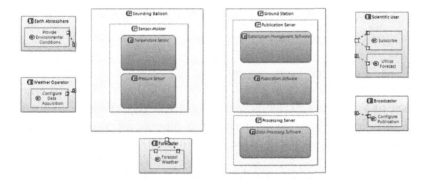

Figure 6.18. *PAB continued. For a color version of the figure, see www.iste.co.uk/roques/arcadia.zip*

We are now going to allocate each Function of the system to one of the Behavior Components. Our example will still be purposefully very simple, perhaps simplistic, for educational purposes. So, we start by allocating the three Physical Functions from the ground station into each Behavior Component. To do this, we use the *Manage Function Allocation* command from the *PAB* palette. Note that the Functional Exchanges are automatically displayed as soon as their target and source Functions are shown on the diagram. By giving the three Functions an optimal size, we quickly come to the fragment in Figure 6.19.

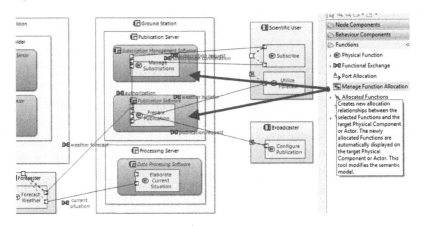

Figure 6.19. *Start of the Functional allocation. For a color version of the figure, see www.iste.co.uk/roques/arcadia.zip*

The Functional Ports are, by default, positioned starting from the upper left corner of each Function, which leads to an undesired cross-over of Functional Exchanges. Yet, there is a very effective command in this instance for asking Capella to automatically position them: *Arrange Connected Ports* on the diagram itself (Figure 6.20).

To simplify the diagram for the rest of the manipulation, we are going to hide the Component Ports, which will also hide the Port allocations on the Actors, by applying the *Collapse Component Ports* filter (Figure 6.21).

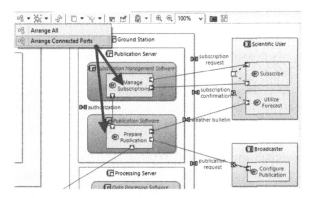

Figure 6.20. *Applying the Arrange Connected Ports command. For a color version of the figure, see www.iste.co.uk/roques/arcadia.zip*

We have one Function left to allocate: "Acquire data". However, we cannot continue further here, because this Function cannot be allocated to several Components. We therefore need to break it down according to the different types of data manipulated: temperature, pressure, etc.

To do this, we must change the diagram type and go back to a *Physical Data Flow Blank (PDFB)*. In this new diagram, we are going to insert the Function to be broken down, as well as all the Functions connected to it, then create as many sub-Functions as types of meteorological data, then work on the data flows, because only the "leaf" Functions may possess Function Ports.

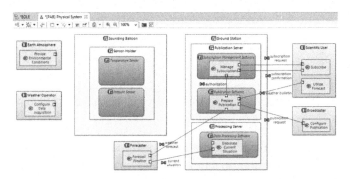

Figure 6.21. *PAB continued with the Component Ports filtered. For a color version of the figure, see www.iste.co.uk/roques/arcadia.zip*

Instead of manually inserting the Functions that we can choose because of the *Insert/Remove Functions* button from the palette, we recall that it is possible to ask Capella to automatically construct the *PDFB* by inserting the Function to be broken down, as well as all those that are connected to it. To do this, we just need to make the diagram contextual with the Function chosen by the properties field of the diagram: *Contextual Elements*.

We first select the "Acquire Weather Data" Function in Capella's *Project Explorer*, then by right clicking, we ask Capella to create a *Physical Data Flow Blank*. Therefore, the diagram thus created will automatically have the name of the selected Function.

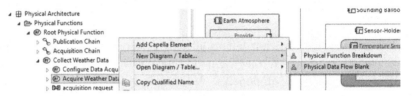

Figure 6.22. *Contextual creation of the PDFB*

We then position the *Contextual Elements* field on this same Function.

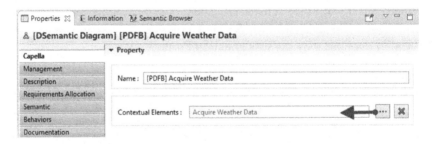

Figure 6.23. *Diagram made contextual using the Function to breakdown*

We just need to ask Capella to refresh the diagram (*F5* key or the *Refresh diagram* button of the upper ribbon) so that the diagram fills automatically. After a few quick manipulations to improve the image, we end up with Figure 6.24.

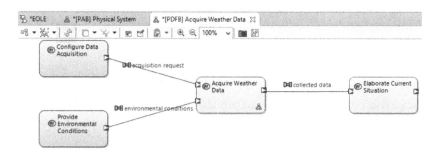

Figure 6.24. *Result from refreshing the contextual diagram*

Now we need to continue our work in breaking down the "Acquire" Function. We remind you that we recommend changing the filling color of the Functions which are broken down, and to make them white to properly differentiate them.

However, unlike what we were able to do when moving from the Operational Analysis to the System Analysis, it is not enough here to shift the Ports from the parent Function to one of the sub-Functions. As a matter of fact, each sub-Function consumes and produces a part of the parent Function's inputs and outputs. We are going to need to call upon the somewhat particular Functions, which are predefined by Arcadia in order to break down or assemble data flows.

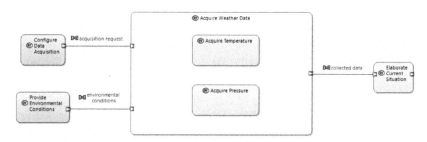

Figure 6.25. *Start of the Functional breakdown*

The collected data at the output of the "Acquire" Function is in part produced by the different sub-Functions (let us not forget that we will also need to acquire the humidity, the wind speed, etc.). We therefore need to add a new Function that will group together these different data. Arcadia defines five types of flow control Functions that we will detail hereafter.

NOTE (Arcadia rule).– As we have already raised, the data flow describes the functional dependencies between Functions, via Functional Exchanges connected to the Function Ports. In certain cases, it may be necessary to define the path conditions more precisely, by using flow control Functions, intermediaries between source(s) and recipient(s):

– to specify a simultaneous broadcast from an exchange source to several recipients, we define a Duplicate Function that transmits the same Exchange Items to all recipients;

– to specify the broadcasting of some of the Exchange Items to each recipient selectively, a Split Function that channels each part to a separate recipient;

– to specify the selection of one among several potential recipients, a Route Function that transmits (generally under conditions) the exchange received on its unique input to one and only one of its outputs;

– to specify the combination of items of several exchanges issued from different sources, a Gather Function to constitute a single Exchange fusing those received from different sources;

– to specify the selection of one source among several, a Select Function, which only channels the exchange issued from the selected source (generally under conditions).

Figure 6.26. Control Functions predefined by Arcadia

In our example, we are therefore going to use *Gather* for the "collected data" output, and *Split* for the "acquisition request" input. We can move the output Port from the parent Function to a *Gather* output and the input Port into a *Split* input. We also need to create new and finer Functional Exchanges for sub-Functions input/output.

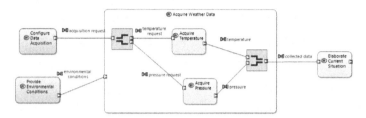

Figure 6.27. *Functional breakdown continued. For a color version of the figure, see www.iste.co.uk/roques/arcadia.zip*

For the minute, we are purposefully going to leave out the environmental conditions issue for which a *Duplicate* appears to be completely indicated. We continue by asking Capella to create a Physical Functional Breakdown diagram (*PFBD*). In this diagram, we can see that the two acquisition sub-Functions, but also the two control Functions, appear automatically because this type of diagram is always up to date. The control Functions appear in gray, rather than in blue or green, and their name has automatically been created by Capella, which will lead us to give them more significant names.

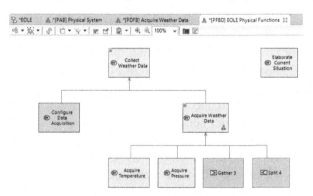

Figure 6.28. *Functional Breakdown diagram (PFBD) . For a color version of the figure, see www.iste.co.uk/roques/arcadia.zip*

We can now go back to the Architecture diagram (*PAB*) and allocate the acquisition sub-Functions to the corresponding sensor. However, this time, the Functional Exchanges do not display automatically as their target and source Functions are missing on the diagram. As a matter of fact, the control Functions are full part Functions: they therefore must also be allocated.

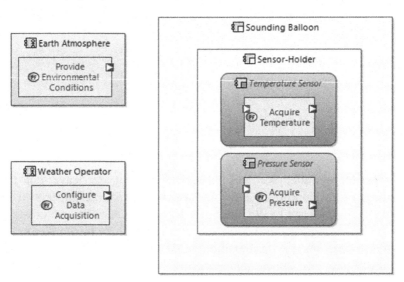

Figure 6.29. *Functional allocation continued*

To allocate a Function, we need a Behavior Component. It is clear that the gathering of collected data must in fact be performed in the balloon, and probably also the splitting of the requests. The only two Behavior Components in the balloon are the different sensors, so we need some transverse intelligence, which could be performed using a specific software Component. This new software Component must also be deployed in turn. Yet, we only have one sensor holder and the structure of the balloon. Then, we are also missing a light hardware support that enables this new software Component to be deployed, such as a Raspberry Pi type nanocomputer, for example. We consequently update the *PAB* on the sounding balloon part.

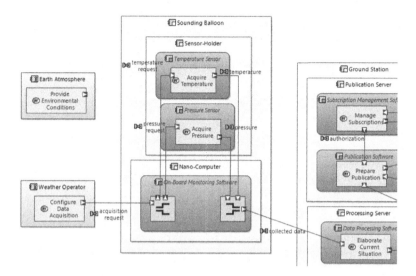

Figure 6.30. *End of Functional allocation. For a color version of the figure, see www.iste.co.uk/roques/arcadia.zip*

NOTE.– What we have just done perfectly illustrates one of the strong points of Arcadia's methodological approach. As a matter of fact, because of the Functional Analysis approach and the precision required in the Functional Exchanges, we were led to create new Physical Functions. Thus, we were forced to consequently complete the structural design by adding new Behavior Physical Components and Nodes in order to finish the necessary allocation of the Functions. In summary, the Functional Analysis enabled us to find the necessary and sufficient architecture Components [VOI 16].

We are now going back to the "environmental conditions" Functional Exchange that we had left out of the Data Flow diagram (*PDFB*). If we add a *Duplicate* type control Function to duplicate this exchange to the two acquisition sub-Functions, we will also need to allocate this additional Function. However, the duplication is done naturally by the "Earth Atmosphere" rather than by designing it inside the sounding balloon. So, this leads the external Actor modeling to be made more complex, without delivering real added value to the architecture model. We are therefore going to use a simpler solution, consisting of duplicating the Functional Exchange by making it part of the same output port. We only lose the precision of simultaneity delivered by the *Duplicate* Function, but to simplify the model.

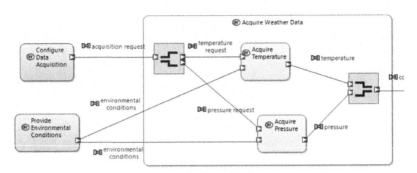

Figure 6.31. *End of work on the Functional Exchanges in the PDFB. For a color version of the figure, see www.iste.co.uk/roques/arcadia.zip*

To reinforce the coherency between the two exchanges, we are going to specify that they transport the same Exchange Item and realize the same Logical Exchange.

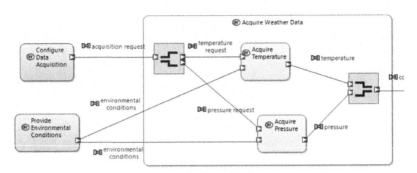

Figure 6.32. *Specifications on the duplicated Functional Exchanges*

If we go back to the *PDFB*, two Functional Exchanges cross over to the left of the acquisition sub-Functions. It is possible to improve the graphic appearance of the intersection by using the *Appearance – Jump Links* property of one of the two Exchanges, as shown in Figure 6.33. By default, the *Jump Links* are disabled (*none*). We need to activate them (*all*) on the selected feature, and then we can modify the style (*semicircle, square, chamfered*) and possibly reverse the jumping direction.

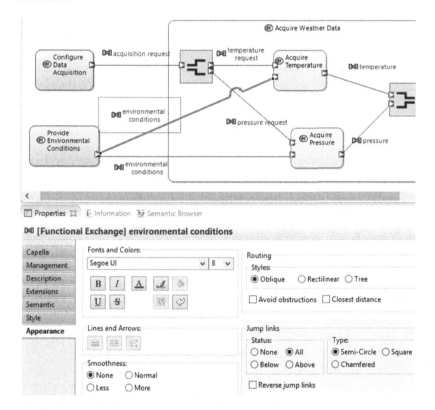

Figure 6.33. *Graphic improvement of the line intersection. For a color version of the figure, see www.iste.co.uk/roques/arcadia.zip*

We now open the *PAB* again: the Functional Exchanges automatically appeared and the diagram is complete.

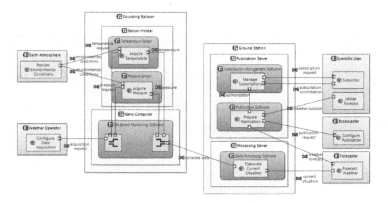

Figure 6.34. *Functional finalization of the PAB. For a color version of the figure, see www.iste.co.uk/roques/arcadia.zip*

6.5. Functional Chains on the Physical level

We had created two Functional Chains on the System level (see section 4.5): "Acquisition Chain" and "Publication Chain". The successive functional transitions from the System level to the Logical level, and then from the Logical level to the Physical level, simply cloned the chains identically. On the Logical level, we had not modified the *data flow*, the Logical Chains therefore continue to be valid. However, on the Physical level, we have broken down the "Acquire Weather Data" Function and detailed the Functional Exchanges with respect to the sub-Functions. It is therefore foreseeable that the "Acquisition Chain" will become invalid, but not the "Publication" one. We check it by inserting the two Chains onto the PAB (Figure 6.35), because of the *Insert Functional Chains* command on the palette.

As predicted, Capella clearly indicates that the Acquisition Chain is now invalid, but not the Publication one, whose constituting items we have not modified. We are therefore going to have to work on the Acquisition Chain in order to make the Physical level valid again. To do this, we must create a specific contextual diagram, called a *Functional Chain Description* (*FCD*), by right clicking on the square in the diagram or on the element in the *Project Explorer* (Figure 6.36).

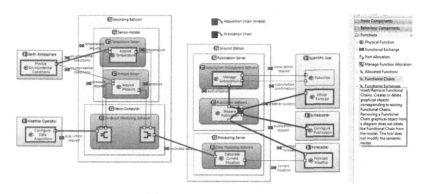

Figure 6.35. *Visualization of the Functional Chains. For a color version of the figure, see www.iste.co.uk/roques/arcadia.zip*

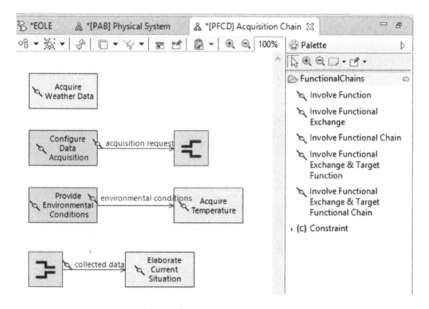

Figure 6.36. *Diagram of Acquisition Chain Description*

The diagram generated thus by Capella clearly shows that there is more than one chain, and that we will need to reconnect the scattered pieces.

We start by removing the link referring to the broken down Function (*Delete from Model* command). Then, we add the missing sub-Function: "Acquire Pressure" (*Involve Function* command). All we need to do now is to connect the sub-Functions using the *Involve Functional Exchange* command. Note that Capella only proposes the existing Functional Exchanges, which prevents errors and accelerates the modeler's work.

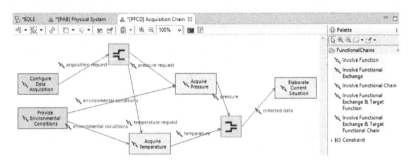

Figure 6.37. *Modification of the Acquisition Chain*

Now we just need to go back to the *PAB* to verify that the Functional Chain has become valid again.

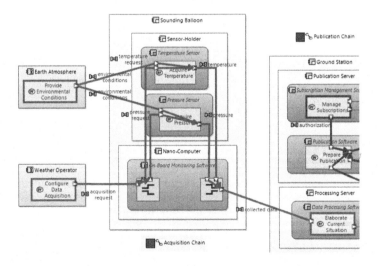

Figure 6.38. *Visualization of the amended Functional Chain. For a color version of the figure, see www.iste.co.uk/roques/arcadia.zip*

On the System level, we indicated that the concept of Functional Chain is particularly useful for running verification/validation tests, as well as for expressing non-Functional constraints, such as latency, criticality, confidentiality, redundancy, etc. On the Physical level, as the Functions that participate in a Chain are all allocated to one single Behavior Physical Component, we can know exactly which Components are necessary and sufficient to ensure the Chain concerned. This information is very important in an incremental delivery process, for example. Capella directly displays the list of Components and Actors implied in the *Semantic Browser* window.

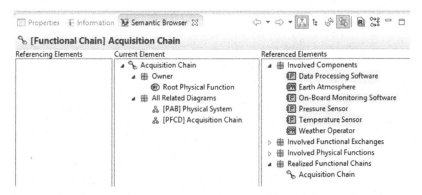

Figure 6.39. *Visualization of the Components implied in a Functional Chain*

6.6. Return to the Physical Components and the structural links

We now return to the *PAB*. We finished the functional analysis and the allocation of Functions to Components. However, there is still a lot of work to do here to finalize the *PAB*, in particular creating the necessary Component Exchanges between the Behavior Physical Components, as well as the corresponding Physical Links between the Node Physical Components.

For simplicity purposes, we are only going to use a particular example to illustrate the approach that needs to be applied to the whole Physical level. We are thus going to focus on the Functional Exchange between the sounding balloon and the ground station: "collected data". To do this, we are first going to clone the *PAB*, and simplify this new diagram by removing all the Actors (*Delete from Diagram* command). This simplified PAB, representing the inside of the EOLE Physical System, is shown in Figure 6.40.

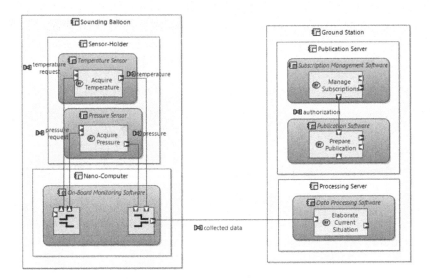

Figure 6.40. *Simplified PAB not showing the Actors. For a color version of the figure, see www.iste.co.uk/roques/arcadia.zip*

The "collected data" Functional Exchange must be allocated to a Component Exchange. To do this, we need to create this Component Exchange between the "On-Board Monitoring Software" and "Data Processing Software" Components. We name it "balloon to ground" and proceed to allocate the Functional Exchange. We can complete its definition by positioning a realization link toward the Logical level Component Exchange.

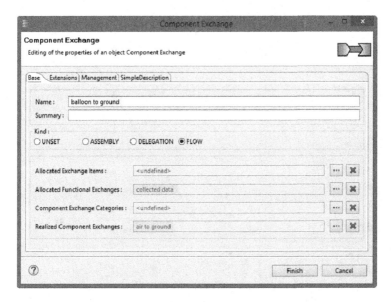

Figure 6.41. *Definition of the Component Exchange*

The result of the allocation appears in the *PAB*, in the same way as for the previous Arcadia levels.

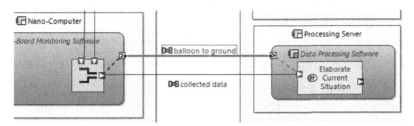

Figure 6.42. *Visualization of the Functional Exchange allocation*

This Component Exchange must in turn be allocated to a Physical Link between Node Physical Components. We could simply create a VHF-type Physical Link between the nanocomputer and the processing server, and then allocate the Component Exchange, as shown in Figure 6.43.

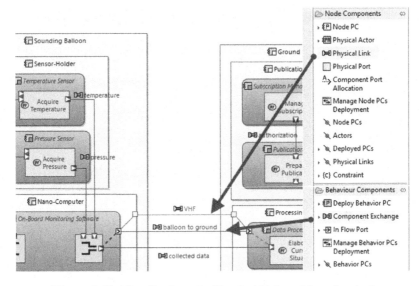

Figure 6.43. *Visualization of a Physical Link and the allocated Component Exchange. For a color version of the figure, see www.iste.co.uk/roques/arcadia.zip*

NOTE (Arcadia rule).– A Physical Link is a means of communication, transport or channeling between two Node Physical Components, used as a support for the Component Exchanges. A Physical Link connects two Physical Ports of two Components. It can directly connect the subcomponents to each other.

A Physical Port is a connection point of a Node Physical Component with its environment. A Physical Port is not oriented. A Physical Port refers to the Behavior Components hosted by its Node Physical Component, which are accessible through it. A Component Port must be allocated to a single Physical Port, as soon as there is a Component Exchange toward the outside of the Component connected to it.

A more complete solution, which allows us to use an additional Arcadia concept further, consists of introducing the radio emission/reception Components, and then to connect a series of Physical Links by means of a Physical Path.

NOTE (Arcadia rule).– A Physical Path is an ordered set of references to Physical Links, defining a continued path likely to channel one or several Component Exchanges between Components not connected by one single Physical Link. A Physical Path refers to the Component Exchanges that it transports.

We start by creating additional Node Components, as well as the three Physical Links to connect them. Note that it is not obligatory to model Behavior Components and Functions inside the new Node Components, because we are focusing on the Physical Links: the modeling may be partial.

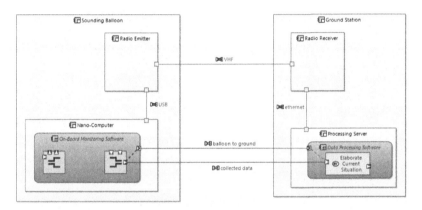

Figure 6.44. *Adding Node Components and Physical Links*

We wish to allocate the "balloon to ground" Component Exchange to the ordered set of Physical Links starting from the nanocomputer and ending with the processing server, rather than the "VHF" Physical link. To do this, we are going to create a Physical Path by successively selecting the three Links and activating a contextual menu by right clicking on the Functional Chain creation model: *Physical Path – Create a Physical Path*. The result is also a new model element represented by a blue square as well as graphic additions on the Links and Physical Ports.

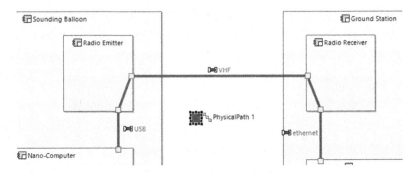

Figure 6.45. *Result of creating a Physical Path. For a color version of the figure, see www.iste.co.uk/roques/arcadia.zip*

We now rename the Physical Path and directly allocate the Component Exchange to it because of the *Property sheet*.

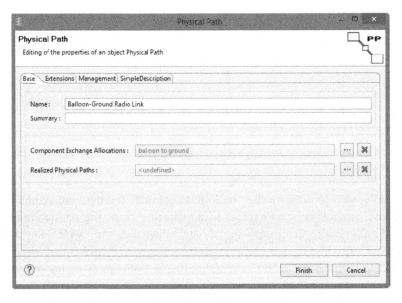

Figure 6.46. *Property sheet of a Physical Path. For a color version of the figure, see www.iste.co.uk/roques/arcadia.zip*

The diagram automatically updates by making the allocation link appear between the Component Ports and the Physical Ports.

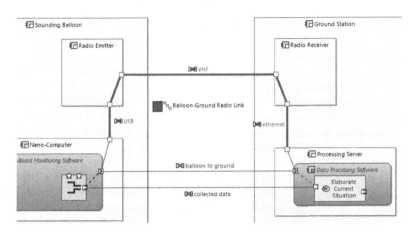

Figure 6.47. *Allocating the Component Exchange to the Physical Path. For a color version of the figure, see www.iste.co.uk/roques/arcadia.zip*

NOTE.– If we want to modify an existing Physical Path, we absolutely must use a specific contextual diagram, called *Physical Path Description* (*PPD*), like for Functional Chains. To create this diagram, we just need to right click on the square in the diagram, or on the model element in *Project Explorer*.

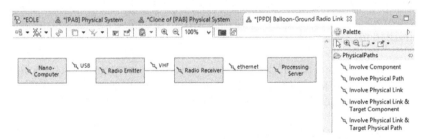

Figure 6.48. *Contextual diagram of the Physical Path Description*

6.7. Integrating Specialty Viewpoints

We recall that the *Specialty Viewpoints* are available in all the Arcadia engineering levels, even if they are mainly used in Physical Architecture. It would be very strange to evaluate the mass and performance of Logical Components whose implementation choices have not been completed. However, a Product Line Viewpoint, or that of Operational Safety, has its rightful place from Logical Architecture onwards.

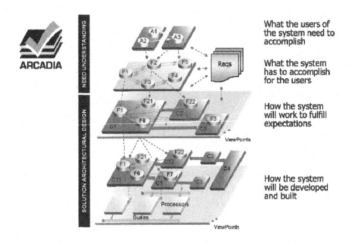

Figure 6.49. *Recall of the architecture levels with the Viewpoints*

So that a modeler can use a specialty Viewpoint, an expert of the specialty and the profession concerned needs to specify it first, then a software developer needs to implement it using Capella Studio [HEL 16].

NOTE.– The subject of developing specialty Viewpoints exceeds the framework of this book. Interested readers may refer to the specialized website, at: wiki.polarsys.org/Capella/Studio.

We simply specify that a Viewpoint first defines the extensions specific to the model elements manipulated by Capella. We are going to take the *Basic Mass* Viewpoint, provided as standard since Capella 1.0, as an example in the rest of this section. This Viewpoint adds additional properties of current mass and maximum mass to the Physical Components (Behavior and Nodes). It also adds a new group of commands in the palette of the Architecture (*PAB*) diagram.

A Viewpoint can then define specific algorithms that can be executed automatically or upon request. The *Basic Mass* Viewpoint automatically calculates the current mass of a containing Component by adding the sum of masses of its contained Components to it. According to the result of these algorithms, the Viewpoint can specify more or less sophisticated conditional graphic annotations. The *Basic Mass* Viewpoint simply compares the current mass of a Component with its maximum mass and makes it red if the threshold has been exceeded.

We are going to illustrate these principles in our case study by focusing on the mass of the sounding balloon. We start by activating the *Basic Mass* Viewpoint on our model. To do this, we first installed the Viewpoint by following the installation procedure explained on Capella Wiki. Then, we must reference the Viewpoint on our model. To do this, we are going to open the *Viewpoint Manager* because of the *Window – Show View – Other – Kitalpha* command. The *Viewpoint Manager* then appears next to the *Semantic Browser*.

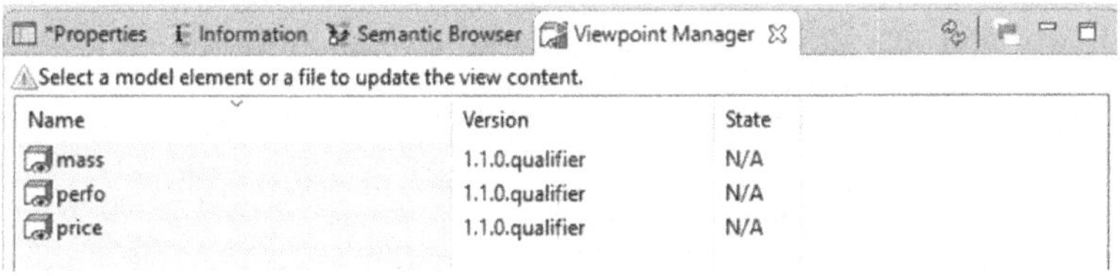

Figure 6.50. *Activating the Viewpoint Manager window*

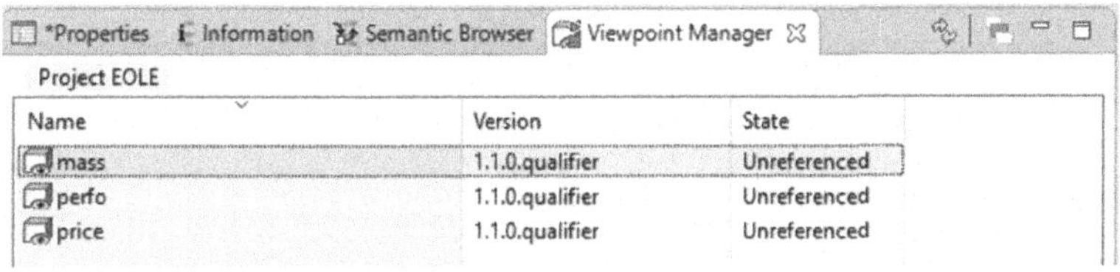

Figure 6.51. *Selecting a model for the Viewpoint Manager*

The correctly installed Viewpoints are visible, but noted as *N/A* (Figure 6.50). Notice that we have installed the three Viewpoints currently provided on the Capella site: *Basic Mass, Basic Performance, Basic Price*. We first have to select a model as indicated in the *Viewpoint Manager* window. We select our EOLE project in Capella *Project Explorer*. The Viewpoints are now noted as *Unreferenced* (Figure 6.51).

To activate a Viewpoint, we just need to right click on *Reference* on the property noted as *Unreferenced*. The chosen Viewpoint then moves to the active state.

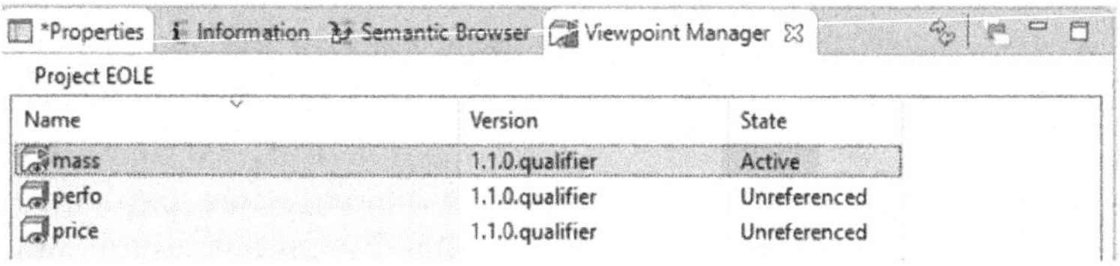

Name	Version	State
mass	1.1.0.qualifier	Active
perfo	1.1.0.qualifier	Unreferenced
price	1.1.0.qualifier	Unreferenced

Project EOLE

Figure 6.52. *Activating the chosen Viewpoint*

We are going to create a new *PAB* in order to show the sounding balloon and its constituents. We add a parachute for regulatory security reasons.

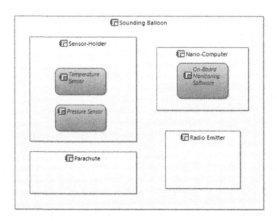

Figure 6.53. *New PAB focused on the sounding balloon*

A Viewpoint is used on a particular diagram by selecting it in the *Layers* command at the top of the diagram.

Figure 6.54. *Selecting the Viewpoint on the PAB*

A new group of commands automatically appears in the palette of the diagram on the right. This basic Viewpoint in fact only adds a single command called *Mass* and which is now applicable to all the Physical Component type model elements.

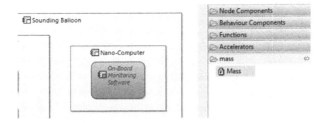

Figure 6.55. *Adding commands in the PAB palette*

Let us suppose that our design brief requires the balloon and accessories set not to exceed a total mass of 1.5 kg. We are going to assign a mass of 500 g to the "Balloon" Node Component, corresponding to its physical sheath, and a maximum mass of 1,500 g.

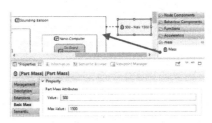

Figure 6.56. *Starting to use a Viewpoint on PAB. For a color version of the figure, see www.iste.co.uk/roques/arcadia.zip*

We continue to assign values to the contained Components by the sounding balloon. When each new value is entered, the current mass of the sounding balloon still increments as much. If this value exceeds the maximum of 1,500, the color of the Component automatically turns red: we will need to find Components that weigh less. But in this case, they may be more expensive and we will need to check that we are not exceeding the maximum price, by applying the *Basic Price* Viewpoint.

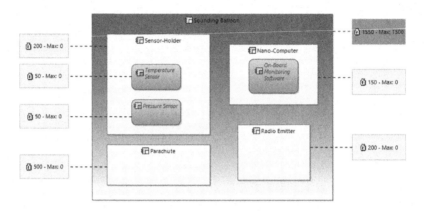

Figure 6.57. *Visualization of the mass Viewpoint effect on a PAB. For a color version of the figure, see www.iste.co.uk/roques/arcadia.zip*

By successively applying several Viewpoints on the same Physical model, the architect will have an effective means of finding the best compromise possible between different architecture solutions, while having the specialty experts work on the same architecture reference.

6.8. Replicable and Replica Elements

A Replicable Element Collection (REC) is a set of model elements, identified as a patron (a model in the current sense of the term) for constructing multiple replicas (or *RPL*), which are maintained in conformity with it.

This concept enables one to take account of the similarity expression needs between model elements. Indeed, it may be necessary to formalize several model elements of the same type and to prevent one from being modified accidentally. This need appears in all types of domains and model elements: Functional Chains need to be repeated for security reasons, networks' generic Components, duplicated processing cards in architecture, etc.

Capella thus enables one to:

– specify, at a given time of the modeling process that a set of model elements must be replicated as a whole;

– constitute a type based on this whole, called REC;

– transform the source elements into a specimen of this type (RPL);

– create other replicas or specimens freely, based on REC;

– maintain the different replicas synchronized with the REC, and propagate possible evolutions from some to others (RPL updates on the REC evolution, propagation of the chosen evolutions of an RPL, etc.).

NOTE.– This mechanism is a little different to that found in software engineering (type/instances), particularly because we generally start by creating a replica, and we then promote it into a REC. Or even because an *REC* may be any set of Capella elements, possibly astride several engineering levels.

We are going to illustrate the possibilities offered by Capella in a small and simple example taken from the EOLE case study. Let us suppose that we want to launch two balloons throughout the day: for example, one at midday and the other at midnight, for which the data will be collected by the same ground station. On a new PAB, we wish to represent the two balloons and their relations with the same receiver station.

We start by isolating the sounding balloon that we want to reuse in a new diagram created for this occasion. The sounding balloon contains Node Components, some of which contain deployed Behavior Components, with Functions allocated to the same. There are also non-connected input and output Ports, both on Functions, the Behavior Components and the Node Components. In particular, we verify that the Functional Ports have associated Exchange Items, even if we are being far from exhaustive on this part started on the System Analysis level (see section 4.9).

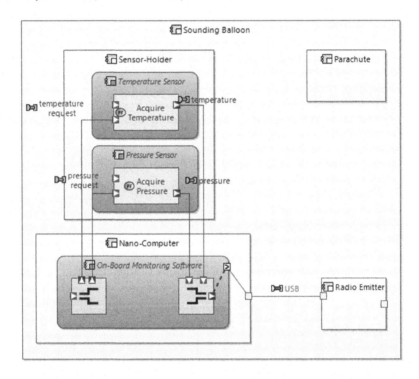

Figure 6.58. *Isolating of the reusable sounding balloon model on a PAB. For a color version of the figure, see www.iste.co.uk/roques/arcadia.zip*

We go back to the *Data Flow* (*PDFB*) diagram where we had broken down the "Acquire Weather Data" Function. A specific filter enables us to display Exchange Items associated with the Functional Exchanges.

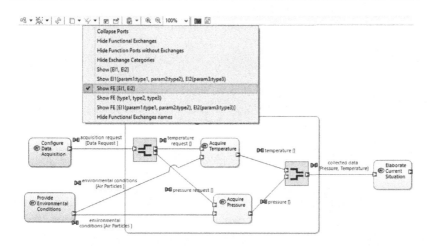

Figure 6.59. *Exchange Items display on the PDFB*

In particular, we can see that the pressure and temperature Exchange Items are missing on the exchanges at the acquisition sub-Functions output. Even when we are going to add them, the corresponding Function Ports will still not be given a type. Indeed, we recall that the association of Exchange Items to a Functional Exchange does not automatically propagate them to Function Ports. Capella proposes a very useful Modeling Accelerator for this: *Propagate Exchange Items to Function Ports.*

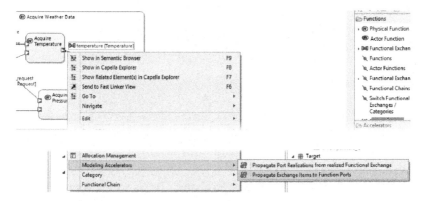

Figure 6.60. *Using a propagation Modeling Accelerator*

The propagation result is easily verified in the *Semantic Browser*.

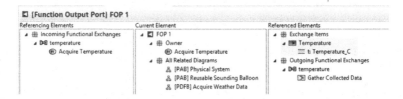

Figure 6.61. *Visualization of the Exchange Items propagation*

NOTE.– It is important to give the Function Ports a type and not only the Functional Exchanges if we wish to reuse the Functions. As a matter of fact, the input/output Function Ports are part of the Function definition, unlike the Functional Exchanges that connect the two Functions.

To illustrate the fact that we can perfectly add new Exchange Items at the Physical level, while referencing the Types created at an upper level, we are going to create a "Temperature Request" and a "Pressure Request" similar to the "Data Request" previously first created on the System Analysis level. For this purpose, we create a new Class Diagram Blank (*PCDB*). We can also insert the "Timestamp" Type coming from the *library*.

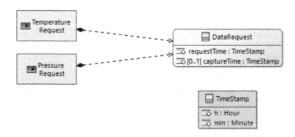

Figure 6.62. *Definition of new Exchange Items at the Physical level*

We can associate these new Exchange Items to the input Ports of the acquisition sub-Functions to end the process. All the Function Ports of the sounding balloon Functions are now associated with at least one Exchange Item.

Good practice consists of also renaming the Component Ports and the Physical Ports of the reusable elements, even if their names do not appear in the diagram. For the radio emitter in our example, the input port is a USB port and the output port is a radio port. We can choose to make these Ports appear in the Capella *Project Explorer* on the left because of the *Customize View* command (they do not appear by default).

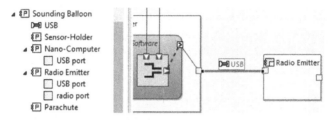

Figure 6.63. *Renaming Physical Ports*

Once this preparatory work has been finished, we can promote this sounding balloon as a Replicable Element (*REC*). To do this, we must be careful when selecting it as well as the model elements that it contains, then by a contextual menu (right clicking), applying the *REC/RPL – Create a REC from selection* command.

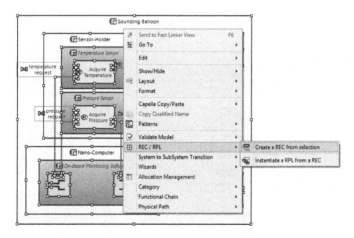

Figure 6.64. *REC creation command. For a color version of the figure, see www.iste.co.uk/roques/arcadia.zip*

Capella then opens a window that allows us to refine the settings of the *REC* creation, by naming it, and by possibly removing the selected model elements (Figure 6.65). For example, we may want to remove the properties brought on by applying a specialty Viewpoint, to make the *REC* more generic. Or otherwise to conserve them to evaluate the effect of redundancy on the mass and the price of the system set, etc.

The replicable element will be positioned in a catalog that is automatically created in the model, or selected by the modeler. It is also possible to specify a conformity property among three possible values: *Black_Box* (default), *Constraint_Reuse, Inheritancy_Reuse.* This property is not yet used in Version 1.1.

NOTE.– Do not hesitate to refer to Capella Online Help, which is very valuable for advanced points, such as the replicable elements: *Help – Help Contents – Capella Guide – User Manual – Replicable Elements.*

Figure 6.65. *Settings window of an REC creation*

The first result of creating the *REC* is seen in the *Project Explorer* on the left, as shown in Figure 6.66.

Figure 6.66. *Result of creating an REC*

So, we can now reuse this *REC* by creating two replicas (*RPL*) of it connected to the ground station in a new *PAB*. In this new diagram, we are going to use the contextual command: *REC/RPL – Instantiate a RPL from a REC*. A window opens in order to configure the replica creation.

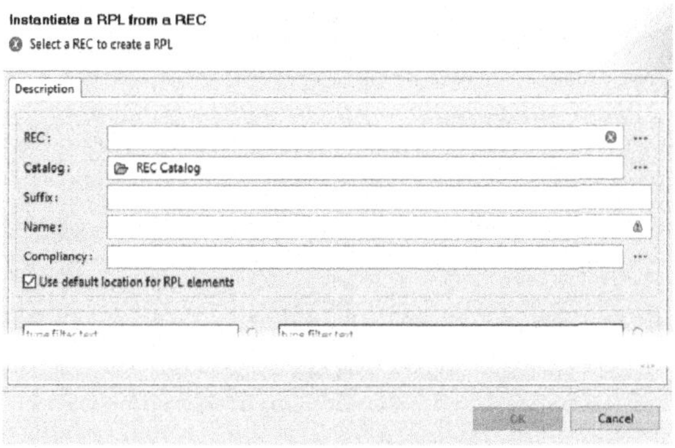

Figure 6.67. *RPL creation window*

We can choose the *REC* to be instantiated by specifying its catalog and adding a suffix to the elements of the replicas requiring it. We can number the sounding balloons, for example, to distinguish them.

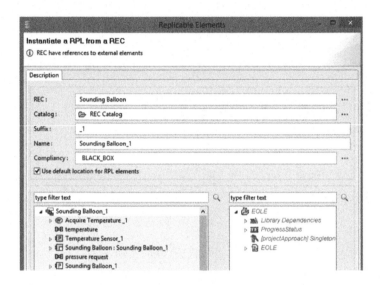

Figure 6.68. *Instantiating the first replica*

Figure 6.69. *Result of creating the RPL in Explorer*

Creating two replicas is clearly manifested in *Project Explorer* because of the suffixes, but also to the acronyms [*REC*] and [*RPL*] that appear behind the name of the model elements (Figure 6.69).

We can now insert both replicas in a new *PAB* and connect them to the ground station. For each replica, we first need to insert the Node Components, and then the Behavior Components deployed, then the allocated Functions. We do not worry about the graphic positioning, as Capella allows us a format copy–paste (*Edit – Copy format*) based on the diagram where the reusable sounding balloon was represented.

Once the two sounding balloon replicas have been inserted, we can insert the ground station. We note that it would have also been possible to create a replicable element for the ground station, particularly if we had wished to represent several stations at different geographical positions.

Thus, in Figure 6.70, we show two sounding balloons and one ground station before connecting the different Components.

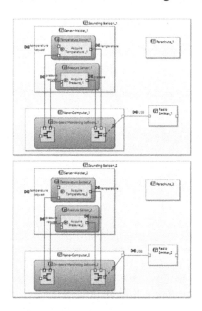
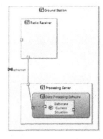

Figure 6.70. *Inserting the RPL into a new PAB. For a color version of the figure, see www.iste.co.uk/roques/arcadia.zip*

As usual, the *Semantic Explorer* clearly indicates the relations between the replicas (*RPL*) and the replicable element (*REC*).

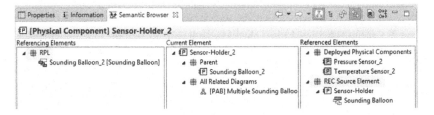

Figure 6.71. *Relation of the RPL and REC in the Semantic Explorer*

Note that the *Semantic Explorer* also indicates that the "temperature" Functional Exchange of each *RPL* always carries the "Temperature" Exchange Item referring to the "Temperature_C (Celsius)" Type, even it that has not been included in the *REC*.

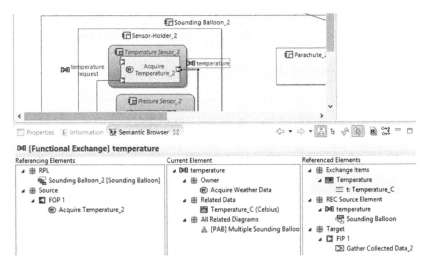

Figure 6.72. *Conserving the link with the Exchange Items and the Types. For a color version of the figure, see www.iste.co.uk/roques/arcadia.zip*

We just need to connect the two sounding balloons to the ground station, as shown in Figure 6.73.

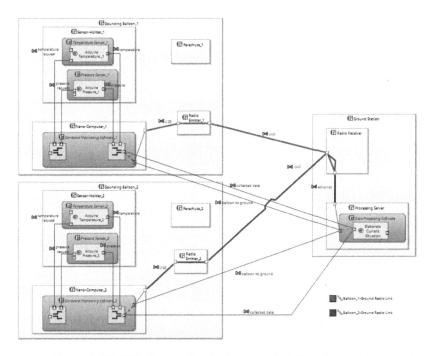

Figure 6.73. *RPL Connection to the ground station. For a color version of the figure, see www.iste.co.uk/roques/arcadia.zip*

NOTE.– To prevent having to manually create the connections again, good practice consists of also creating an *REC* for the ground station, even if we only instantiate it once. As a matter of fact, when a pair of *REC* is connected by Functional and Component Exchanges and Physical Links, it is possible to propagate these connections between the corresponding *RPL* via the *Update Connections* command.

7

Complete Example of Modeling
with Capella: EPBS

7.1. Main concepts and diagrams

Capella integrates methodological guidance under the form of *Activity Explorer*. This lists the different activities and diagrams that can be made on the engineering level concerned; in this case, this is namely *EPBS (End Product Breakdown Structure)*. Figure 7.1 describes the activities and diagrams that are possible.

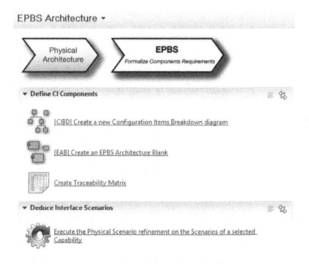

Figure 7.1. *Methodological activities and diagrams on the "EPBS" level*

NOTE.– This level is much lower than the four previous ones, in terms of concepts, diagrams and methodological activities. In certain recent Arcadia presentations, it is no longer even represented as an engineering level, but rather as an "industrial organization" viewpoint on physical architecture.

7.2. Moving from the Physical level to the EPBS level

This level aims to use the Physical Architecture to deduce the conditions that each component must fulfill to satisfy the design constraints and architecture choices, identified in the previous phases ("what is expected of the provider of each component"). The Physical Components are often gathered into Configuration Items that are larger and more practical to manage, in terms of industrial organization and responsibilities. The classic problem consists of asking ourselves whether we are going to make the component, reuse a similar one, buy it off the shelf, or subcontract it out, etc.

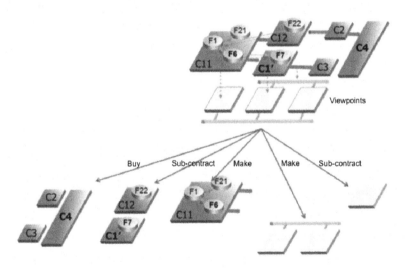

Figure 7.2. *From the Physical Architecture to the EPBS. For a color version of the figure, see www.iste.co.uk/roques/arcadia.zip*

NOTE.– Unlike the previous levels, Capella does not currently propose any transition to initialize EPBS based on the Physical Architecture.

7.3. Configuration Item

A Configuration Item is a part of the system, to be acquired or designed and produced, in as many copies as required by the Physical Architecture, and which will be assembled with other items to constitute each of the system's copies. Several physical Configuration Items may be gathered into a Prime Item, thus defining the product tree. The system is most often at the root of the tree defined thus.

This general concept can thus be shrunk into:

– System CI: system type configuration item;

– Prime Item CI: configuration item that can be broken down;

– CSCI: software type configuration item;

– HWCI: hardware type configuration item;

– NDI: non-developed configuration item;

– COTS: Component Off The Shelf configuration item.

In our case study, we have known from the beginning that the system will contain two Subsystems: an airborne acquisition Subsystem for which the state of the art consists of using a sounding balloon inflated in helium and a ground processing Subsystem. It is therefore natural to make two *Prime Items* on the first level. We will then list the necessary Configuration Items in the form of a product tree, and therefore on a breakdown diagram (*CIBD*).

For example, we are going to decide that we will buy the sounding balloons off the shelf (*COTS*), as well as the sensors and the parachute, but we will make the on-board software. We could also decide to subcontract the on-ground software applications. With all these hypotheses, and by using fictitious product names, the simplified product tree could resemble the following diagram (Figure 7.3).

NOTE.– The colors were added manually; all the Configuration Items have the same color by default.

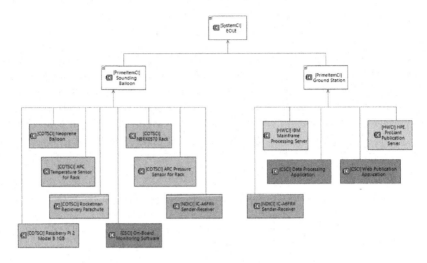

Figure 7.3. *Simplified example of EPBS for EOLE. For a color version of the figure, see www.iste.co.uk/roques/arcadia.zip*

For each Configuration Item, we can add a unique identifier, as well as specifying the traceability with the Physical Components. For example, we will open the property sheet of the "IBM Mainframe processing server".

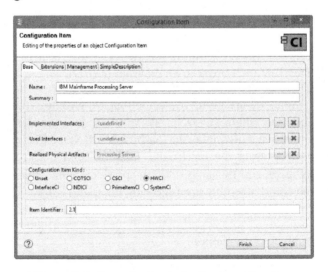

Figure 7.4. *Property sheet of a Configuration Item*

7.4. Traceability between Configuration Items and Physical Components

This traceability can be established in different ways. Of course, we can open the property sheet of each Configuration Item and fill the *Realized Physical Artifacts* field, but also use other possibilities:

– edit the Traceability Matrix proposed in the *Activity Explorer*;

– create an *EPBS Architecture Blank* (EAB);

– use the *Fast Linker* window.

We are going to illustrate these three possibilities one by one; however, the simplest and the most efficient is the Traceability Matrix.

We start by creating the *EAB* Architecture Blank diagram. It allows us to create or insert the Configuration Items, then add the realization relations and to show the Physical Components inside the *CI*. We sketch the diagram on the ground station for now.

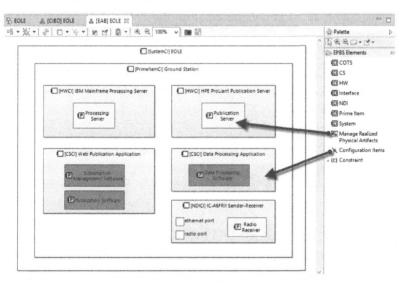

Figure 7.5. *Start of the Architecture Blank diagram (EAB). For a color version of the figure, see www.iste.co.uk/roques/arcadia.zip*

NOTE.– The Configuration Items can realize one or several Physical Components, but also Physical Ports and Links. We have shown it in the previous diagram for the "IC-A6FRII sender-receiver" NDICI.

Another way to proceed consists of using the *Fast Linker*. This is a particular window, which was created when Capella was opened at the bottom left. If it was closed, we just need to activate it again by the *Window – Show View – Fast Linker* menu.

We can send an item into the *Fast Linker* by sliding/moving from the *Project Explorer* or the *Semantic Browser*, or by activating a contextual command on a model element of type: right click/*Send to Fast Linker View* (F6).

If the model element can accept links, it remains visible in the *Fast Linker*. Otherwise, it is rejected. As soon as another element is put into the *Fast Linker*, Capella verifies if it can be linked with the first one and then automatically creates the link or rejects it. If several links are possible, a window of choice is proposed to the user.

We show an example for creating the automatic realization link into two steps for the temperature sensor, as shown in Figure 7.6.

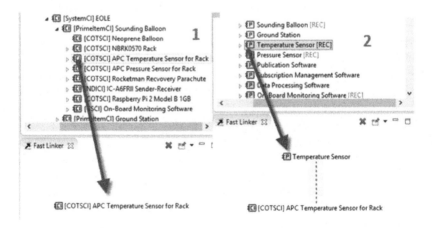

Figure 7.6. *Use example of the Fast Linker*

But as we said, the most efficient is probably to work directly on the Traceability Matrix, calculated by Capella according to the existing relations and that can be edited easily. We go back into *Activity Explorer* and we click on *Create Traceability Matrix*. The matrix obtained is rather raw and contains all the traceable physical elements as columns: Node and Behavior Components, Ports and Physical Links.

NOTE.– The matrix takes all the physical elements into account, both those of the REC and those of RPL. The elements that we do not need must be filtered so as to make the matrix more usable.

Therefore, we are going to hide some of the columns that are not useful because of the *Hide/Show table columns* command, which is applied by right clicking on the matrix.

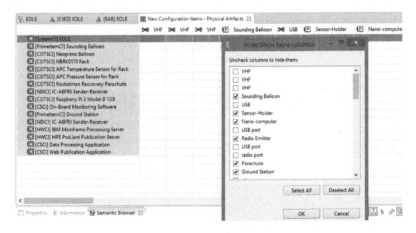

Figure 7.7. *Preparing the EPBS/PA traceability matrix*

We can also hide the lines corresponding to the *PrimeItem* type items to obtain the following matrix, which is very clearly truncated to the right.

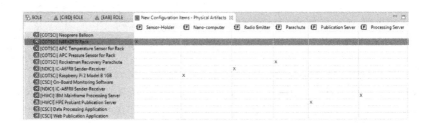

Figure 7.8. *Filling the EPBS/PA traceability matrix*

We therefore finish our work on the EOLE case study in the hope that it encourages you to delve deeper into the various possibilities offered by Capella.

It is clear that we did not have the sufficient space in this first book to go further into some of the tool's advanced features; however, we endeavor to do it by yourself with the precious help of the Online help, as well as the Users Forum available on the Capella Website.

Figure 7.9. *Capella Users Forum*

Conclusion

Capella's Key Strengths

Summary of key strengths

We hope that the previous chapters, and the work on the case study in particular, will have convinced you of Capella's numerous key strengths.

We will attempt to briefly summarize the main points that distinguish it from other UML/SysML modeling tools on the market:

– integrated methodological guide (*Activity Explorer*);

– *Semantic Browser;*

– integrated validation of Arcadia methodological rules (*Validate Model*);

– help with managing complexity (ability to hide complexity, filters, calculated links, accelerators, etc.);

– iterative and incremental interlevel transitions;

– iterative and incremental system/subsystem transitions;

– semantic color grid.

In short, not only does Capella efficiently know a modeling language, but also a methodological approach (Arcadia).

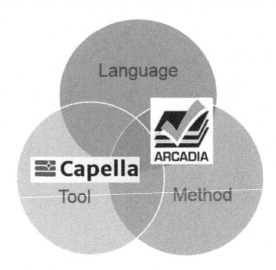

MBSE with Arcadia/Capella

The Capella ecosystem

With a lack of satisfying solutions on the market, the Thales group chose to pour its in-house modeling technologies into Open Source in order to create a de facto standard, to hatch an ecosystem and to contribute to funding the innovation.

Logically, the Eclipse foundation, whose tools already underlied the arsenal of engineers at Thales, became involved. This foundation constitutes an Open Source community recognized in software development. Historically, under the aegis of technology providers, the foundation replaced users at the forefront, especially in today's industry. Eclipse working groups were created for this purpose, including PolarSys (www.polarsys.org), who initially sought to entrench the works carried out within the framework of OPEES and *TopCased*, another Open Source modeling platform for on-board systems (driven by Airbus in particular).

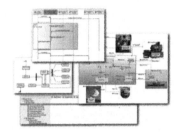

Discover Capella

Capella is a model-based engineering solution
that includes a graphical modeling workbench that
helps engineers build better architectures. Capella
provides the tools necessary for engineering-wide
collaboration through shared reference
architectures and the ability to understand and
define complex architectures.

The Polarsys Website: https://www.polarsys.org/

With the support of Obeo, a French SME that is well known in the Eclipse world, Thales proceeded to implement the whole of its technological platform and its modeling components within the *Kitalpha* project in Open Source to provide a complete technological foundation.

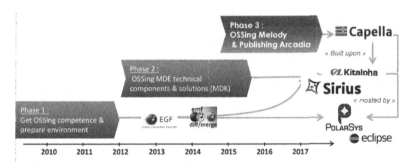

The Open Source implementation by Thales

Thales' goals are numerous:

– to be able to share models with clients or subcontractors for communication or even contracting purposes;

– to guarantee the continuity of the investment already made through de facto standardization;

– to share the development and maintenance costs with other partners;

– to continue to improve the method and the tool because of greater and more varied experience feedback.

The ultimate motivation is for it to constitute a complete ecosystem with users, technology providers, service providers, academics and researchers, etc. The first ecosystem was set up within the framework of the aforementioned Clarity [BOU 16] project, which was started in September 2014 to be finished at the end of 2017, with the stakeholders, as shown in below figure.

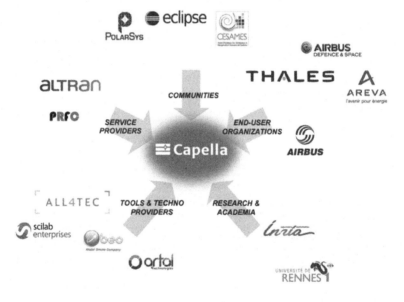

The stakeholders of the initial ecosystem, Clarity

There is a European follow-up to this Clarity project on the cards with many additional stakeholders, and which should kick off at the beginning of 2018.

Moreover, a *Capella Industry Consortium* based on the existing *Papyrus IC* model is currently being created in order to bring all of the parties involved in the Capella ecosystem together, with open governance. For more information, the reader can visit the Website: www.polarsys.org/capella/industry-consortium.html.

Goals

Capella IC provides to its members an open governance on several axes related to Capella tool, add-ons and underlying technologies:

- **Knowledge Sharing:** case studies, technology watch, private exchange workshops on N&N.
- **Promotion:** Promote Capella as a leading solution; provide material to executive.
- **Product Management:** Requirements co-creation; discuss the roadmap.
- **Development of the Community:** Collaboration between research/academia, suppliers and end-users.
- **Joint Development Financing:** Coordinate investments to reduce development times, risks and costs, and maximize ROI.

The goals of the Capella Industry Consortium

Bibliography

[BON 16] BONNET S., "Capella Team: Live collaborative modeling with Sirius", *SiriusCon,* Paris, France, 2016.

[BOU 16] BOUDJENNAH C., "Capella: the Birth of an Industrial Ecosystem", *CSD&M,* Paris, France, 2016.

[CAS 18] CASSE O., *SysML in Action with Cameo Systems Modeler,* ISTE Press, London and Elsevier, Oxford, 2018.

[HEL 16] HELLEBOID M., LANGLOIS B., "Viewpoint: the making of Customizing Capella with Capella Studio in 20 minutes", *EclipseCon France,* Toulouse, France, 2016.

[ROQ 04] ROQUES P., *UML in Practice: The Art of Modeling Software Systems Demonstrated through Worked Examples and Solutions,* Wiley, 2004.

[VOI 16] VOIRIN J.L., BONNET S., EXERTIER D. *et al.,* "Simplifying (and enriching) SysML to perform functional analysis and model instances", *INCOSE IS,* Edinburgh, Scotland, 2016.

[VOI 18] VOIRIN J.L., *Model-based System and Architecture Engineering with the Arcadia Method,* ISTE Press, London and Elsevier, Oxford, 2018.

Index

Printed in the United States
By Bookmasters